Cruzian Mystic Books / Sema Institute of Yoga
P.O.Box 570459
Miami, Florida, 33257
(305) 378-6253 Fax: (305) 378-6253

The author is available for group lectures and individual counseling. For further information contact the publisher.

Ashby, Muata
The Ancient Egyptian Buddha: The Ancient Egyptian Origins of Buddhism ISBN: 1-884564-61-5

Temple of Shetaut Neter-Aset
INTERNET ADDRESS:
www.Egyptianyoga.com
E-MAIL ADDRESS:
Semayoga@aol.com

TABLE OF CONTENTS

FOREWORD

This book is a compilation of several sections of a larger work, a book by the name of *African Origins of Civilization, Religion, Yoga Mysticism and Ethics Philosophy*. It also contains some additional evidences not contained in the larger work that demonstrate the correlation between Ancient Egyptian Religion and Buddhism. This book is one of several compiled short volumes that has been compiled so as to facilitate access to specific subjects contained in the larger work which is over 680 pages long. These short and small volumes have been specifically designed to cover one subject in a brief and low cost format.

This present volume, ***The Ancient Egyptian Buddha: The Ancient Egyptian Origins of Buddhism***, formed one subject in the larger work; actually it was one chapter of the larger work. It was felt that this subject needed to be discussed because even in the early 21st century, the idea persists that Buddhism originated only in India independently. Yet there is ample evidence from ancient writings and perhaps more importantly, iconographical evidences from the Ancient Egyptians and early Buddhists themselves that prove otherwise. This handy volume has been designed to be accessible to young adults and all others who would like to have an easy reference with documentation on this important subject. This is an important subject because the frame of reference with which we look at a culture depends strongly on our conceptions about its origins. in this case, if we look at the Buddhism as an Asiatic religion we would treat it and it's culture in one way. If we id as African [Ancient Egyptian] we not only would see it in a different light but we also must ascribe Africa with a glorious legacy that matches any other culture in human history and gave rise to one of the present day most important religious philosophies. We would also look at the culture and philosophies of the Ancient Egyptians as having African insights that offer us greater depth into the Buddhist philosophies. Those insights inform our knowledge about other African traditions and we can also begin to understand in a deeper way the effect of Ancient Egyptian culture on African culture and also on the Asiatic as well. We would also be able to discover the glorious and wondrous teaching of mystical philosophy that Ancient Egyptian Shetaut Neter religion offers, that is as powerful as any other mystic system of spiritual philosophy in the world today.

Ancient Relationship Between Egypt, Ethiopia and India

Introduction

Indian culture is one of the most fascinating and rich cultures of human kind. Indian history spans several thousands of years and encompasses several periods of spiritual philosophy. This course is a survey of the various religions that have been practiced in India from ancient times beginning with the Indus Valley civilization which flourished about c. 3000 to the present day.

Where is India and What is its Physical Proximity to Kamit {Egypt}?

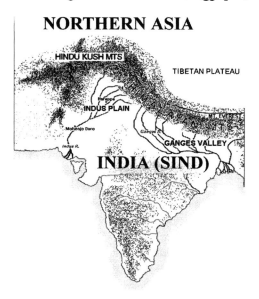

Above: Map of Ancient India.

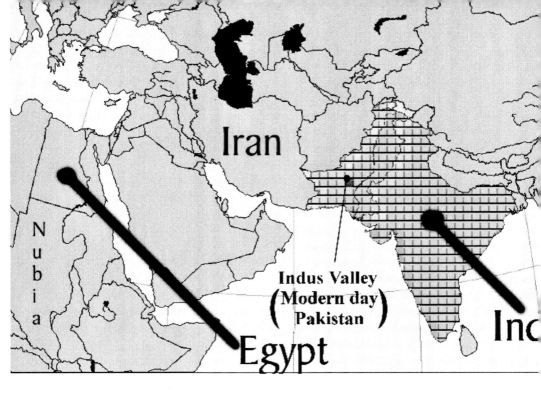

Above: Map of Ancient India.
Above: Map of Southern Asia and Eastern Africa

The Ethiopian Kush or Cush refers to the kingdom of Nubia[1], which according to the ancient writings of Egypt as well as the writings of the classical Greek historians is the source of both Ancient Egyptian civilization as well as Indian civilization.

Evidence of Contact Between Ancient Egypt and India

The following are statements from the writings of Greek classical writers who traveled the ancient world and reported about the peoples they saw and the lands where they lived as well as their interrelationships. [Highlighted sections by Ashby]

"I shall speak of the king who reigned next, whose name was Sesostris[i] He, the priests said, first of all proceeded in a fleet of ships of war from the Arabian gulf along the shores of the Indian ocean, subduing the nations as he went, until he finally reached a sea which could not be navigated by reason of the shoals. **Hence he returned to Egypt, where, they told me, he collected a vast armament, and made a progress by land across the continent, conquering every people which fell in his way.**

In this way he traversed the whole continent of Asia, whence he passed on into Europe, and made himself master of Scythia and of Thrace, beyond which countries I do not think that his army extended its march."

- History of Herodotus (Greek historian 484 B.C.E.)
- [i] Senusert I, reigned in 1,971. B.C.E.

"All the Indian tribes I mentioned ... their skins are all of the same color, much like the Ethiopians."

-History of Herodotus (Greek historian 484
B.C.E.)

"And upon his return to Greece, they gathered around and asked, "tell us about this great land of the Blacks called Ethiopia." And Herodotus said, **"There are two great Ethiopian nations, one in Sind (India) and the other in Egypt."**

-Diodorus (Greek historian 100 B.C.)

"From Ethiopia, he (Osiris {Asar})[ii] passed through Arabia, bordering upon the Red Sea to as far as India, and the remotest inhabited coasts; he built likewise many cities in India, one of which he called Nysa, willing to have remembrance of that (Nysa) in Egypt where he was brought up. At this Nysa in India he planted Ivy, which continues to grow there, but nowhere else in India or around it. **He left likewise many other marks of his being in those parts, by which the latter inhabitants are induced, and do affirm, that this God was born in India.** He likewise addicted himself to the hunting of elephants, and took care to have statues of himself in every place, as lasting monuments of his expedition."

- Diodorus (Greek historian 100 B.C.)
[ii] Reigned c. 10,000 B.C.E.

Some modern day Hindus continue to believe Egypt is their ancestral home.

-
> **"Some Hindus claim the Nile to be one of their sacred rivers; they also regard as sacred the Mountains of the Moon (in Uganda-Congo) and Mount Meru (in Tanzania).** Both in India and in the

Indianized Kingdoms, Southern Mount Meru was regarded as the mythical dwelling place of the Gods. Each of these statements reflect millennia old relationships between the blacks of Africa and South Asia. The Ethiopian Kebra Negast regarded Western India as a portion of the Ethiopian Empire. **"Murugan, the God of mountains", the son of the mother Goddess is a prominent and typical deity of the Dravidian India.** It is interesting to note that at least 25 tribes in East Africa worship "Murungu" as supreme God, and like the Dravidian God Murugan, the African Murungu resides in sacred mountains."

-From: U.P. Upadhyaya
"Dravidian and Negro-African International Journal of Dravidian Linguistics"
v.5,No 1 January 1976, p 39.

Indian Archeologists Discover Contact and Correlations Between Ancient Egypt and India

What follows is a portion of the research contributed by Indian scholars based on archeological excavations, working in India and Egypt on the question of contact and interaction between Ancient Egypt and India. The maritime trade between Ancient Egypt and India is known to have lasted longer and to have been more reliable than the over-land route through Asia Minor (Afghanistan, Iran, Iraq and Syria.). Therefore, during the periods when Egyptian rule over Asia Minor waned, due to wars and the influx of Indo-European peoples from the North of Asia, the contact between Ancient Egypt and India was maintained by sea.

"Direct contact between the two countries (India and Egypt) during this period (Pharaonic Egypt 3400-525 B.C.) is suggested by some highly specialized artifacts which are found in India as well as in Egypt but which, surprisingly, are absent in the vast West Asian region between-Afghanistan, Iran, Iraq and Syria."[2]

The material evidence of such contact includes:

"HEAD-RESTS: Indian head-rests found at some Neolithic sites such as T. Narsipur, Hemmige, and Hallur-all in Karnataka in south India-may be consigned to dates in the first half of the second millennium B.C. on the basis of radio-carbon tests. Curiously, they occur only in south India[3] and have no parallels elsewhere in tile subcontinent except for a solitary contemporaneous specimen from Chanudaro assigned to Jhukar levels[4] of circa 1800 B.C.

In Egypt, similar head-rests belonging to a period spanning the pre-Dynasty Period to Roman times have been discovered. A number of them are made of wood but in some, intended for royalty and the aristocracy, costlier materials such as ivory and lapis lazuli are employed. Egyptian headrests occur in a variety of forms. Incidentally, certain tribes of Africa[5] and India use wooden head-rests even today.[6] Strikingly identical head-rests have also been carved in rock bruisings at Piklilial in Karnataka (India), which site has, interestingly also yielded specimens in pottery belonging to the Neolithic period."

The obvious cultural connection between Ancient Egypt and India led to several aspects of cultural interaction so it is no surprise to find many artifacts, concepts of philosophy and other factors that can be directly correlated. These factors of correlation solidify our understanding of early Indian culture as a development of or strongly influenced by Ancient Egyptian-African culture and civilization. That allows us to have a deeper understanding of the Indian practices and a better understanding of their original intent. One of the most important and fundamental items of correlation is the concept and symbol known as "OM".

General Indian History

Indian history may be divided into three broad periods, Ancient India, Medieval India and Modern India. Ancient India spans from the time of the Indus Valley Culture 2500 B.C.E. to the fall of Harshavardhan (reign - 604 - 647 A.C.E.). The ancient period includes the time of the emergence of the Aryans and Buddhism in India. The medieval period of Indian history begins with the Rajput period. The first Rajput kingdoms are attested in the 6th century, and the Rajputs rose to prominence in Indian history in the ninth and tenth centuries A.C.E. This time was an era that has been characterized as one of chivalry and feudalism. The constant fighting of the Rajputs weakened them. This weakening allowed the Turks (foreigners) to mount victorious campaigns in India using military force or intrigue (duplicity and deceit). The period of Modern India begins with the coming of the Europeans, when Vasco da Gama landed at Calicut. He sailed via the Cape of Good Hope and arrived in 1498 A.C.E. This event marked the beginning of the modern (European era) in Indian history.

Religion in prehistoric and ancient India

The major movements in the prehistoric period of ancient India relate to the Indus Valley Civilization, 2,800 B.C.E.–1800 B.C.E., also referred to as Harappan Civilization of the Indus Valley or more recently Saraswati civilization; and the emergence of the Aryan culture, Hinduism, Buddhism, and Jainism.

The existence of civilization and limited practice of organized religion in Indian history can be dated to the Indus Valley culture whose ruins reveal an Indian civilization dating from 2,500 B.C.E. The Indus Valley culture was the author of architecture, sculpture and rudimentary organized religious practices.

It is believed by many Indologists that migrating shepherds, who are referred to as "Aryans", entered India from the central area of Asia. They in turn pushed the Dravidian inhabitants (who had created the Indus Valley culture) to the south. The Aryans instituted the Sanskrit language and writing and also instituted the caste system. The Indus Valley area is today within the country known as Pakistan, as well as parts of India and Afghanistan.

Early in the first millennium B.C.E. Hinduism and Jainism emerged as distinct forms of religious practice but related to the prehistoric (Dravidian) indigenous Indian religious practice and influenced by the Vedic tradition. Hinduism emerged as an amalgamation of the preexisting Indian religious practice and the Aryan Vedic tradition. The word "Hinduism" is a Western term. The religion called Hinduism is actually referred to by the Hindus themselves as "Sanatana-Dharma," which means "the eternal law" or "the path or righteous actions or way of life." The word derives from an ancient Sanskrit term meaning "dwellers by the Indus River," a reference to the location of India's earliest known civilization in what is now Pakistan.

The Brahmins (Brahmanism) emerged as a priestly class based in the Vedic Tradition. It was this tradition that implemented the caste system in ancient India. The Upanishadic tradition, which is an aspect of Hinduism, emerged as a development or reworking of and perhaps a departure from the Vedic tradition. The Vedanta tradition constitutes an aspect of the Upanishadic traditions which focuses on the distillation or concentration on the most important teachings of the Upanishads, seeing them as developments of the Aryan Vedas. Jainism emerged in conjunction with Hinduism incorporating the teachings of its founder, Mahavira. Later, Buddhism emerged, making use of Hindu teachings, such as Dharma, but without the Divine iconography or usage of divinities. It represents a departure from the rigidity and ritualism of Brahmanism and the Vedic tradition.

Introduction to Buddhist Spirituality

In the book Egyptian Yoga Vol. 1 I compiled a very basic introduction to Buddhism. That was followed up with a more substantial exploration in the book Egypt and India. In a teaching manual and book called Introduction to Religious Ethics and the World Religions I presented an expanded overview of Buddhist religion and philosophy. Buddhism is a religion that began in India in Association with Ancient Egypt and later spread throughout India and was later spread throughout Asia even while its practice was reduced in India. The historical Buddha, Siddhartha Gautama (c. 563- c. 483 B.C.E.) was mythically reputed to have been a prince who gave up his royal life to seek after spiritual evolution. The traditional story of his life relates that he turned to the Brahmins, the Hindu Monks, and practiced austerities, but felt that he was obtaining minimal results from his efforts. Prior to Buddha, there were similar teachings such as those of the Jains and those of the "Brahmins" and "Sanyasa" (renunciation), where one was supposed to renounce the apparent reality as an illusion, were taken to extremes wherein some followers would starve themselves to the point of death in order to achieve spiritual experience. Others became deeply involved with the intellectual aspects of philosophy, endlessly questioning; Teachings such as that of non-violence, of the Jain religion, which stressed not harming any creatures were understood by some as not moving so as not to step on insects or not breathing in without covering the mouth so as not to kill insects or microorganisms. The myth goes on to say that he then turned inwards and discovered a new path to attain spiritual salvation. It was called the middle way. He developed the Eight-Fold Path. Thus the central doctrines and rituals of the Buddhist tradition center on the concepts espoused in the Eight-Fold Path. (Ashby, 1995, 2002).

After Buddha died his followers met to decide how best to follow his legacy and promote the teaching. Over the next several hundred years there were at least four Buddhist councils where the canon of the teaching, including Dhamma, [ethics, righteous action discipline for promoting purity] was discussed. However, differences led to the creation of no less than 18 different schools of Buddhist philosophy. Out of the original 18 or more sects of early Buddhism only the Theravada survives. All others that we see in the world today developed later in history. The more conservative monks were accused of not taking into account the needs of the general populace and so a new sect was created to serve the needs of the laity. That new sect was called Mahayana (Ashby, 2002).

It is well known and documented that Emperor Ashoka of India, upon becoming a Buddhist convert, was instrumental in the dissemination of the Buddhist teachings throughout the known ancient world. He sent Buddhist missionaries throughout India and to various countries. There are also several iconographical evidences and separate historical records from the time of Ashoka that link Buddhism with Neterianism [Ancient Egyptian Religion] and especially with the Temple of Menefer (Memphis) in Egypt. Buddhist records show that early Buddhists had visited Memphis and had set up a settlement there. Henceforth Buddhism begins to develop similar iconographies including the Divinity sitting on the lotus, and also lotus friezes similar to those of Ancient Egypt appear in Buddhist art. Another similarity specifically with Tibetan Buddhism is the usage of a transition or after death guidance text. The Bardo Thodol, is a Tibetan text that is sometimes referred to as the Tibetan Book of the Dead. Bardo Thodol literally means, "Liberation through Hearing in the State of Bardo." The Bardo Thodol is a funerary text, not unlike the Pert m Hru text of Ancient Egypt, that explains the experiences of after death consciousness during the interval or intermediate period called bardo in the Tibetan Book of the Dead and Duat in the Ancient Egyptian Book of the Dead. In the book Search for the Buddha by Charles Allen, the author documents the Buddhist connection to Ancient Egypt as follows. The Buddhist/Indian ruler had a practice of setting up pillars with inscriptions attesting to his following the Buddhist principles and other edicts. One was discovered that unequivocally shows that ancient Egypt and India were associated (Ashby, 2002).

The views on causality, mindfulness, monasticism, salvation, purity, and ethics in the Theravada school begin in "The Noble Truth of the Cause of Suffering: The cause of suffering is Ignorance (Avidya). Ignorance causes a person to develop desires and the suffering due to frustrations and mental agitations associated with those desires leads to suffering. The answer to this dilemma is to be found in statement #7 of The Noble Eight-fold Path: Right Mindfulness is learning how to be aware of everything that one does at all times, not acting automatically, reacting to events as an animal. Theravada Buddhism is focused on monasticism but it also has a role for the lay people. The goal of the monk is to attain Nibbana through proper reflection and meditation. The role of lay people is to serve the needs of the monks and to perform good deeds so as to improver their karma. Purity is attained through 'merit making' activities that improve karma (kammatic Buddhism). According to Theravada human life is governed by Karma. Therefore, it is necessary to perform good deeds to purify the Karma and thereby move closer to attaining the goal of nirvanic salvation (Ashby, 1995, 2005).

Tantric Buddhism developed from the Mahayana school of Buddhism. As in Mahayana, the concept of ethics is important, requiring the practitioner to karmicly purify themselves. In Mahayana Buddhism the focus of philosophy and practice is on bodhicitta or purified mind. A person possessing such a mind is called Bodhisattva. Part of the discipline of purity means practicing virtues. The Bodhisattva has six virtues or perfections (paramitas) to be practiced and perfected: patience, generosity, morality, meditation, wisdom and energy. There are two divisions of Tantric Buddhism, the Tibetan and the Shingon. Tantric Buddhism holds that it can promote a faster means to attain the goal of Nirvana through special tantric techniques and esoteric initiation. In terms of soteriology, the Buddhist concepts of salvation are different in terms of the school of practice. In Mahayana practice is more oriented towards the goal of salvation which may be defined as "deliverance from an undesirable state or condition." In Theravada the goal is freedom or liberation from reincarnation or samsara, the cycle of rebirth, by attaining Nirvana. The Vajrayana school claims it can lead a person to Buddhahood or "enlightenment" in a very short time, perhaps even a single lifetime.

Zen Buddhism is the Japanese name for Buddhism, mostly related to Mahāyāna Buddhism. Mahāyāna Buddhist schools were adopted in Japan along with their meditation practice that is called Dhyana in India. Zen Buddhist practice accentuates the role of zazen or sitting meditation in the task of pursuing spiritual enlightenment. That practice is also done to benefit others so the practice also emphasizes compassion. Traditional accounts tell of how Zen was brought to China and founded by an Indian Buddhist monk by the name of Bodhidharma. The Japanese Rinzai school is renowned due to its emphasis on the experience of sudden enlightenment as well as the use of special methods like the koan for achieving that goal. The Zen teacher D.T. Suzuki, who was also a philosopher and Japanese Rinzai master, held that a Zen satori or awakening was the goal of the Zen training. In Buddhist practice Paramita refers to the perfection state or culmination state of certain disciplines. Bodhisattvas practice and cultivate the Paramita disciplines for the purpose of moving from sensuous living (Samsara) to Nirvana (Enlightenment).

Buddhism and its Main Teachings

B uddhism gained adherents not by force but by appeal and free choice. With the championing of King Ashoka, Buddhism was spread throughout India and almost the entirety of India was Buddhist by the 6th century A.C.E.. The Hindu revival in the 8th century and the coming of Islamic armies in the Indian subcontinent led to the decline of Buddhism in India in the medieval period.

Today there are several schools of Buddhist thought and practice. Theravada Buddhism has traditionally determined a difference between the practices that are suitable for monks and those for a layperson and nuns. Even though the capacity for some attainment by laypersons is acknowledged, it is given less significance in Theravada Buddhism than in the Mahayana and Vajrayana traditions.

Theravada is the oldest surviving school of Buddhism from the early period schools. It has become the main religion of Sri Lanka as well as continental Southeast Asia including China, Myanmar, Laos, Cambodia, and Thailand). It is also growing in Australia and Singapore. Theravada is sometimes condescendingly referred to as Hinayana with the associated intended meaning of "Inferior Vehicle" as opposed to Mahayana (the "Greater Vehicle"). However, that interpretation of the term is widely viewed as either derogatory or inaccurate. The more accurate meaning is "little vehicle" since the more intensive practices are only suited for a minority while the Mayahana practices are more designed for a wider participation and are therefore less restrictive and intensive.

Theravada practice promotes a concept called Vibhajjavada (Pali), which literally means "Teaching of Analysis." This teaching makes use of critical thinking and investigation methods as opposed to imagination or blind faith. In this way the aspirant is convinced of the teaching via logical reasoned thought processes and through experiences in the practice that gradually lead them to higher openings in consciousness and the goal of Theravada practice. In Theravada practice the goal is to achieve a state of consciousness called Arahant which literally means "worthy one", or the "winner of Nibbana"). Having attained that goal there is no more reincarnation and the goal of holiness in life is achieved and there is no more to be achieved or done; this is the goal of life. This is the same state of enlightenment that was achieved by the Buddha himself. When Mahayana Buddhism came into existence the Mahayana practitioners came to regard the Arahant state as a level of consciousness lower than that which was attained by the Buddha himself.

A layperson's role in the practice has been centered around 'merit making' activities that improver their karma (kammatic Buddhism). Activities that promote merit include: offering basic necessities to the monks, such as offering food, donations for monasteries and temples. Other merit making activities include lighting candles or burning incense in front of Buddha images, as well as chanting merit-making or protective verses from the **Abhidharma** or Pali Canon of the Theravada Buddhist teaching.

Kammatic Buddhism rationalizes the seemingly random fate, blind or a capricious divinity. A person can get over feeling aggrieved or wronged by their present negative condition or fortunes. Those conditions can now be understood as their karmicly merited result of past wrong actions and/or dispositions either in the present lifetime or in a former life. Thus, all good conditions and prosperities arise as a fruit from the past good (ethic) deeds.

Pāramitā (*Sanskrit*) or **Parami** (*Pāli*) means "Perfection" or "Transcendent" attainment; they are disciplines for purification and enlightenment.

In Theravada Buddhism, the Ten Perfections (*Paramis*) are; (original terms in Pali) [7]

1. *dāna parami* : generosity, giving of oneself
2. *sila parami* : virtue, morality, proper conduct
3. *nekhamma parami* : renunciation
4. *panna parami* : transcendental wisdom, insight
5. *viriya parami* : energy, diligence, vigour, effort
6. *k□anti parami* : patience, tolerance, forbearance, acceptance, endurance
7. *sacca parami* : truthfulness, honesty
8. *aditthana parami* : determination, resolution
9. *metta parami* : loving-kindness
10. *upekkha parami* : equanimity, serenity

In Theravada Buddhism the monastic discipline can be divided generally into two roles. One role is the usually urban tradition of scholar monk. The other role is the usually rural meditation monk. These two types of monks serve the people as conductors of ceremonies and through religious teaching in basic Buddhist morality and philosophy.

The Mahayana school of Buddhism developed beginning in the 1st century A.C.E. Scholars regard the official emergence of Mahayana Buddhism as being around the mid 2nd century A.C.E. during the convening of the 4th Buddhist Council by the Kushan emperor Kanishka. This council formally confirmed the establishment and validation of Mahayana Buddhism. The Mahayana scriptures began to be put into writing about the 1st century B.C.E. Some of those scriptures were presented if they had been authentic sermons of the original Buddha which had been previously hidden. The Perfection of Wisdom sutras are important scriptures of that time. The Mahayana school of Buddhism is less austere and conservative than the Theravada school. Its main tenets include:[8]

- **Universalism**, Everyone will become a Buddha.
- **Enlightened wisdom**, as the main focus of realization.
- **Compassion** through the transferal of merit.
- **Salvation**- as opposed to **Liberation**- supported by a rich cosmography, including celestial realms and powers, with a spectrum of Bodhisattvas, both human and seemingly godlike, who can assist followers.

Thus, in Buddhism it is held that all sentient beings can be free of suffering as the original practitioner, Gautama did, in spite of their Biological sex, age, or caste. The practice in what is referred to as "Philosophical Mahayana" is inclined towards focusing Universality, enlightened wisdom, and compassion and does not incline towards supernatural interpretations. The "Devotional Mahayana" does tend towards supernatural constructions and focuses on salvation in other-worldly realms.

In Mahayana Buddhism the focus of philosophy and practice is on bodhicitta. Bodhicitta means developing a mind that is characterized by great compassion but also a mind that incorporates wisdom (prajna) in order that it may realize emptiness. With such a mind the Buddhist practitioner does realize (attain) the ultimate goal of the practice, Buddhahood or full enlightenment. Enlightenment here refers to an omniscient mind that is completely free of suffering and unaffected by the causes of suffering. Such a mind has the capacity to work tirelessly and dynamically for the good of all living beings. A person possessing such a mind is called Bodhisattva. Part of the discipline of purity means practicing virtues. The Bodhisattva has six virtues or perfections (paramitas) to be practiced and perfected: patience, generosity, morality, meditation, wisdom and energy.

The Vajrayāna sect of Buddhism is also known or referred to as *Tantric Buddhism, Tantrayana, Diamond Vehicle, Mantrayana, Esoteric Buddhism*, or *True Words Sect*. Tibetan Buddhism was in the past referred to by some people as "Lamaism" but that is a misunderstanding of the term since the position of the Lama in Tibet is *Teacher*. It is regarded as a third major Yana or 'vehicle' (path) of Buddhism. The other vehicles of Buddhism are the Theravada and the Mahayana. Vajrayana is regarded as a development out of Mahayana Buddhism. The different designation is not due to philosophical differences with Mayanana but rather to the incorporation of added techniques (upaya). Upaya means 'skilful means'. Vajrayana practice in the present has two major sub-groups or schools. These include Tibetan Buddhism and Shingon Buddhism. Tibetan Buddhism is practiced in:[9]

- Tibetan Buddhism, found in Tibet, Bhutan, northern India, Nepal, southwestern and northern China, Mongolia and, various constituent republics of Russia that are adjacent to the area, such as: Amur Oblast, Buryatia, Chita Oblast, Tuva Republic, and Khabarovsk Krai. There is also Kalmykia, another constituent republic of Russia that is in fact the only

Buddhist region in Europe, located in the north Caucasus.
- Shingon Buddhism, found in Japan

The *Bardo Thodol*, is a Tibetan text that is sometimes referred to as the Tibetan Book of the Dead. Bardo Thodol literally means "Liberation through Hearing in the State of Bardo." The Bardo Thodol is a funerary text, not unlike the *Pert m Hru* text of Ancient Egypt, that explains the experiences of after death consciousness during the interval or intermediate period called bardo. The intermediate period is the time between death and rebirth. The Bardo Thodol is to be recited over a person who is dying or recently deceased person by lamas. The text can be recited over an figure of the deceased.

The *Bardo Thodol* intermediate states after death are divided into three bardos (Which are further subdivided):

1. the *chikhai bardo* or "bardo of the moment of death"
2. the *chonyid bardo* or "bardo of the experiencing of reality"
3. the *sidpa bardo* or "bardo of rebirth".

The *Bardo Thodol* also discusses three more bardos: "life" (or ordinary waking consciousness), "dhyana" (meditation), and "dream".

Vajrayana Buddhism is different in that it claims to offer path to enlightenment that is accelerated. The accelerated process is achieved via the use of special tantric techniques. Those techniques are practical helps to promote spiritual development. Thus, while the Theravada or Mahayana schools promise enlightenment over a period of many lifetimes, the Vajrayana school can lead to Buddhahood or enlightenment a very short time, perhaps even a single lifetime. Vajrayana Buddhists don't consider the Theravada or Mahayana teachings and practices to be invalid, but that they are slower pathways. One other nuance of difference in the schools is that in Mahayana and Vajrayana the goal is to attain Buddhahood. In Theravada the goal is freedom or liberation from reincarnation or samsara, the cycle of rebirth, by attaining Nirvana. In Tibetan Buddhism the special tantric techniques are transmitted esoterically (through energetic force of teacher at initiation)

As in Mahayana Buddhism, Tibetan Buddhism accepts a Pantheon or divinities, manifestations or bodhisattvas, Buddhas, and Dharmapala. The Dharmapala are mythic fearsome protectors of Dharma. Bodhisattvas are those beings who can or have attained enlightenment but who and can escape reincarnation (cycle of death and rebirth) but choose not to in order to stay on earth to help others to reach nirvana or Buddhahood out of their compassion.

Tibetan Buddhism can be differentiated from other Tantric Buddhism schools in that Tibetan Buddhism holds the belief that some lamas can reincarnate in lineages known as *tulkus.* One important reincarnated Tibetan leader is the Dalai Lama. Also, Tibetan Buddhism holds that spiritual masters can recover a lost practice or hidden scriptures (*termas*) from ancient times. They also believe that a Buddha, such as Padmasambhava, the saint that instituted Tibetan Buddhism in the Himalayas can be visible in human form.[10]

Meditation is a special practice in Tibetan Buddhism that includes special techniques and may be accompanied by special chanted mantras and hand gestures (*mudras*). One of the famous chants is "om mani padme hum" by Chenrezig. Several meditation methods are used by different Tantric traditions. Some examples include: *dzogchen, mahamudra*. Some practitioners also study and construct diagrams called *mandalas,* that have special cosmic meaning, which help in promoting inner spiritual progress.

Those who not been initiated can perform acts that gain for them good merit. They can perform rituals such as water offerings, food and flower offerings, chanting prayers (may use prayer wheel or prayer flag), or religious pilgrimages. Non-initiates may light butter lamps at the local temple or pay monks to light them for them. Villagers can also gain merit by participating in or observing cham dances.

Tibetan Buddhism has four main traditions (the suffix *pa* is comparable to "er" in English):[11]

- Nyingma(pa), *The Ancient Ones*, the oldest and original order founded by Padmasambhava himself
- Kagyu(pa), *Oral Lineage*, headed by the Karmapa and having four major sub-sects: the Karma Kagyu, the Tsalpa Kagyu, the Baram Kagyu, and Pagtru Kagyu; as well as eight minor sub-sects, the most notable of which are the Drikung Kagyu and the Drukpa Kagyu; and the once-obscure Shangpa Kagyu, which was famously represented by the 20th century teacher Kalu Rinpoche.
- Sakya(pa), *Grey Earth*, headed by the Sakya Trizin, founded by Sakya Pandita 1182–1251CE
- Geluk(pa), *Way of Virtue*, also known as *Yellow Hats*, whose spiritual head is the Ganden Tripa and whose temporal head is the Dalai Lama, who was ruler of Tibet from the mid-17th to mid-20th centuries.

And one minor one:

- Jonang(pa), suppressed by the rival Gelukpas in the 1600s and once thought extinct, but now known to survive in Eastern Tibet.

In Tantric Buddhism there is also an ecumenical movement called *Rime*.

Zen Buddhism is the Japanese name for Mahāyāna Buddhism. Mahāyāna Buddhist schools were adopted in Japan along with their meditation practice that is called Dhyana (ध्यान) in India. The same practice was later accepted in China as Ch'an (禪), and then in Korea, and Vietnam. Zen Buddhist practice accentuates the role of zazen or sitting meditation in the task of pursuing spiritual enlightenment. That practice is also done to benefit others so the practice also emphasizes compassion. In the west the teaching was in the past regarded as just a type of sitting meditation practice. However, Zen Buddhism encompasses a complete school of Buddhist practice and religious philosophy.

In the latter part of the 20th century, Zen Buddhism became known internationally and there are centers in several countries around the world. Traditional accounts tell of how Zen was brought to China and founded by an Indian Buddhist monk by the name of Bodhidharma.[12] Bodhidharma has been associated with the Shaolin Temple and the creation of the traditions and schools of Kung Fu and T'ai Chi Ch'uan.

The Japanese Rinzai school is renowned due to its emphasis on the experience of sudden enlightenment as well as the use of special methods like the koan for achieving that goal. The Zen teacher D.T. Suzuki, who was also a philosopher and Japanese Rinzai master, held that a Zen *satori* or awakening was the goal of the Zen training. The differences between Buddhist traditions that developed in India and those that developed in China, Korea, and Japan was in the manner that the way of life differed from the Indian Buddhists. In India, the Buddhists lived as mendicant holy beggars while farther east, in China the society lent itself to a temple format which allowed a training-center system to develop. The temple was supported by mundane tasks performed by the abbot and all the monks. Those mundane tasks include housekeeping, food gardening or farming, architecture, carpentry, administration, and the practice of folk medicine.

Zen Buddhism developed in China and several teachings from Taoism and Confucianism. Zen Buddhism refers to itself as the Buddha Heart School, tracing the lineage back in time to the Buddha through the Flower Sermon in which the Dharma was first communicated. Zen and Mahayana Buddhist traditions, in general, put more stress on the Paramitas (Path of Perfection) practices and less stress Eightfold Path practices. However, the basic knowledge of the Eightfold Path is necessary.

Pāramitā (*Sanskrit*) or **Parami** (*Pāli*) means "Perfection" or "Transcendent" attainment; they are disciplines for purification and enlightenment. In Buddhist practice Paramita refers to the perfection state or culmination state of certain disciplines. Bodhisattvas practice and cultivate the Paramita disciplines for the purpose of moving from sensuous living (Samsara) to Nirvana (Enlightenment).

In Mahayana Buddhism, the Perfection of Wisdom (*Prajna-paramita*) Sutra and Lotus (*Saddharmapundarika*)

Sutra list the Six Perfections as; (original terms in Sanskrit)[13]

1. *Dāna* paramita: generosity, giving of oneself
2. *Sila paramita* : virtue, morality, proper conduct
3. *K☐anti paramita* : patience, tolerance, forbearance, acceptance, endurance
4. *Virya paramita* : energy, diligence, vigour, effort
5. *Dhyāna paramita* : one-pointed concentration, contemplation
6. *Prajña paramita* : wisdom, insight

The later <u>Ten Stages</u> (*Dasabhumika*) Sutra lists another four;

7. <u>*Upāya paramita*</u>: skillful means
8. <u>*Pranidhana*</u> *paramita*: vow, resolution, aspiration, determination
9. *Bala paramita*: spiritual power
10. <u>*Jñana*</u> *paramita*: knowledge

Ethics in Buddhism

In **Buddhism** ethics are referred to as Dhamma (similar to the Hindu Dharma). For (Mahayana Buddhism) laypeople, ethics are called the Pancasila which includes: no killing, no stealing, no lying, no sexual misconduct, and no intoxicants. Some Mahayana groups also include prohibitions against other items like gambling. So a layperson must take a vow to refrain from taking part in the actions listed here in order to prevent the accumulation of negative karma. However, Buddhist nuns and monks take several more vows (called vinaya). The **Vinaya** ('discipline') is the framework for right conduct in the monastic Buddhist community, also referred to as sangha. The teachings for right conduct of the Buddha, also Buddha dharma may be thought of as encompassed by two broad groupings: 'Vinaya', or discipline and 'Dharma' or doctrine.

In Buddhism, the code of disciplines for monks and nuns consists of 227 rules for the monks (bhikkhus) and 311 rules for the nuns (bhikkhunis).
The rules are arranged into sections:[14]

- Parajika - Rules entailing expulsion from the Sangha (defeat)
- Sanghadisesa - Rules entailing an initial and subsequent meeting of the Sangha (communal meetings)
- Aniyata - Indefinite rules
- Nissaggiya Pacittiya - Rules entailing forfeiture and confession
- Pacittiya - Rules entailing confession
- Patidesaniya - Rules entailing acknowledgement
- Sekhiya - Rules of training

- <u>Adhikarana Samatha</u> - Rules for settling disputes

Buddhist ethics are composed of hypothetical imperatives rather than categorical imperatives. The difference is that the Buddhist concept does not promote abstaining from stealing and killing simply just for the sake of doing what is correct. The true purpose is to achieve a certain goal, and that goal is to attain enlightenment.

Hinayana (Sanskrit: "small vehicle"; Chinese: 小乘 *Xiǎoshèng*; Japanese: *Shōjō*; Vietnamese: *Tiểu thừa*) is a term that was invented by the Mahayana practitioners, that came into public appearance around the 1st century A.C.E. One understanding of the term is that it relates to a more controlled and narrow practice of Buddhism as opposed to Mahayana (Sanskrit: "large vehicle") which relates to the practices of the laypeople and therefore means that the rules are relaxed so that more people can practice. Some practitioners and scholars see the Hinayana as relating to the Early Buddhist Schools, while other practitioners and scholars view Hinayana as additionally cognate the Theravada tradition, a modern sect. **Mahayana Buddhists** emphasize the bodhicitta principle. This idea holds that a person should not seek enlightenment for their own sake alone, but rather for "all sentient beings." Buddhism is often regarded as one of the most peaceful religions. Some writers have noted that a Buddhist holy war has never occurred. However, contemporary politics in Sri Lanka has produced Buddhist monks who regularly urge military action against that island's Tamil minority. Other historical examples could be cited, e.g. from Tibet and its relation to the Bön faith.[15] Nevertheless, of the modern religions of the world Buddhism is indeed the least advocate for violence and one of the most vocal advocates for tolerance and peace. In Buddhism, ethics are fundamentally considered to be based on wisdom arrived at through human reflections as opposed to divine revelation. So in Buddhism, the teaching are not regarded as supernaturally derived and therefore are to be embark on willingly out of a person's own volition as opposed to being compelled by "commandments." In Buddhism, egoism (desire, craving or attachment) is due to ignorance and therefore ignorance is considered to be the reason for all suffering. Therefore, compassion, kindness and equanimity are thus regarded as the pure essence of human nature. Thus, in Buddhism altruism is regarded as a fundamental and intrinsic feature of human nature.

Qualities of Buddha Dharma

In Buddhism Dhamma also refers to the teaching of the Buddha itself. So practice of Buddhist wisdom is part of the ethical training and practice of Buddhism. Buddhist teaching includes six supreme qualities:[16]

1. Svakkhato The Dhamma is not a speculative philosophy, but is the Universal Law found through enlightenment and is preached precisely. Therefore it is excellent in the beginning (Sīla ... Moral principles), Excellent in the middle (Samadhi. . . Concentration) and excellent in the end (Pań ña . . . Wisdom),
2. (Samditthiko) The Dhamma can be tested by practice and therefore he who follows it will see the result by himself through is own experience.
3. (Akāliko) The Dhamma is able to bestow timeless and immediate results here and now, for which there is no need to wait till the future or next existence.

4. (Ehipassiko) The Dhamma welcomes all beings to put it to the test come and see for themselves.
5. (Opāneyiko) The Dhamma is capable of being entered upon and therefore it is worthy to be followed as a part of one's life.
6. (Paccattam veditabbo viññūnhi) The Dhamma can be perfectly realized only by the noble disciples (Ariyas) who have matured and enlightened enough in supreme wisdom.

Buddhists follow the qualities because they believe that by knowing them they will be able to attain happiness and peace through the Dhamma. Therefore, each person is completely responsible for putting the principles into real practice.

The Neterian Religion Origins
of Indian Buddhism

Where is the land of Egypt?

A map of North East Africa showing the location of the land of *Ta-Meri* or *Kamut,* also known as Ancient Egypt.

The Ancient Egyptians lived for thousands of years in the northeastern corner of the African continent in the area known as the Nile River Valley. The Nile River was a source of dependable enrichment for the land and allowed them to prosper for a very long time. Their prosperity was so great that they created art, culture, religion, philosophy and a civilization which has not been duplicated ever since. The Ancient Kamitans (Egyptians) based their government and business concerns on spiritual values and therefore, enjoyed an orderly society which included equality between the sexes, and a legal system based on universal spiritual laws.

The *Egyptian Mystery System* is a tribute to their history, culture and legacy. As historical insights unfold, it becomes clearer that modern culture has derived its basis from Ancient Egypt, though the credit is not often given, nor the integrity of the practices maintained in the new religions. This is another important reason to study Ancient Egyptian Philosophy, to discover the principles which allowed their civilization to prosper over a period of thousands of years in order to bring our systems of government, religion and social structures to a harmony with ourselves, humanity and with nature.

The flow of the Nile brought annual floods to the Nile Valley and this provided irrigation and new soil nutrients every year that allowed for regular crops when worked on time. This regularity and balance of nature inspired the population to adopt a culture of order and duty based on cosmic order: Maat. This idea extends to the understanding of Divine justice and reciprocity. So if work is performed on time and in cooperation with nature, there will be order, balance and peace as well as prosperity in life.

Kamit (Egypt) is located in the north-eastern corner of the continent of Africa. It is composed of towns along the banks of the Hapi (Nile River). In the north there is the Nile

Delta region where the river contacts the Mediterranean Sea. This part is referred to as the North or Lower Egypt, "lower," because that is the lowest elevation and the river flows from south to north. The middle of the country is referred to as Middle Egypt. The south is referred to as Upper Egypt because it is the higher elevation and the river flows from there to the north. The south is the older region of the dynastic civilization and the middle and north are later.

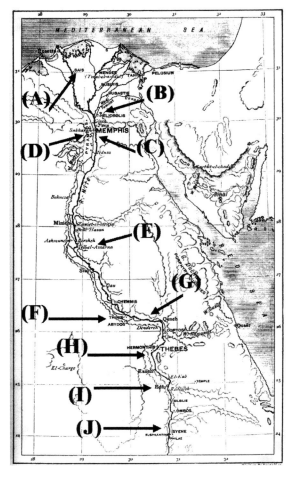

The Ancient Egyptian cities were related to certain divinities and their respective religious theologies.

The Land of Ancient Egypt-Nile Valley - The cities wherein the theology of the Trinity of Amun-Ra-Ptah was developed were: A- Sais (temple of Net), B- Anu (Heliopolis- temple of Ra), C-Men-nefer or Hetkaptah (Memphis, temple of Ptah), and D- Sakkara (Pyramid Texts), E- Akhet-Aton (City of Akhnaton, temple of Aton), F- Abdu (temple of Asar)-Greek Abydos, G- Denderah (temple of Hetheru), H- Waset (Thebes, temple of Amun), I- Edfu (temple of Heru), J- Philae (temple of Aset). The cities wherein the theology of the Trinity of Asar-Aset-Heru was developed were Anu, Abdu, Philae, Denderah and Edfu.

The Sphinx and its contemporary architecture throughout Kamit give us the earliest history, the earliest recorded evidence of the practice of advanced religion anywhere in the world. The Sphinx has now been proven to be the earliest example of the practice of religion in human history, 10,000 BCE.

The next religion appears in India at about 2,500 to 3,000 BCE. We have shown in the book *African Origins* that there was a direct relationship between the Indians and the Ancient Egyptians/Ancient Africans, so much so that the basic tenants of Hinduism and Buddhism can be directly correlated to Shetaut Neter.

When Was Ancient Egyptian Civilization?

KAMIT

(Ancient Egypt)

A Brief History of Ancient Egypt

Christianity was partly an outgrowth of Judaism, which was itself an outgrowth of Ancient Egyptian culture and religion. So who were the Ancient Egyptians? From the time that the early Greek philosophers set foot on African soil to study the teachings of mystical spirituality in Egypt (900-300 B.C.E.), Western society and culture was forever changed. Ancient Egypt had such a profound effect on Western civilization as well as on the native population of Ancient India (Dravidians) that it is important to understand the history and culture of Ancient Egypt, and the nature of its spiritual tradition in more detail.

The history of Egypt begins in the far reaches of history. It includes The Dynastic Period, The Hellenistic Period, Roman and Byzantine Rule (30 B.C.E.-638 A.C.E.), the Caliphate and the Mamalukes (642-1517 A.C.E.), Ottoman Domination (1082-1882 A.C.E.), British colonialism (1882-1952 A.C.E.), as well as modern, Arab-Islamic Egypt (1952- present).

Ancient Egypt or Kamit, was a civilization that flourished in Northeast Africa along the Nile River from before 5,500 B.C.E. until 30 B.C.E. In 30 B.C.E., Octavian, who was later known as the Roman Emperor, Augustus, put the last Egyptian King, Ptolemy XIV, a Greek ruler, to death. After this Egypt was formally annexed to Rome. Egyptologists normally divide Ancient Egyptian history into the following periods: The Early Dynastic Period; The Old Kingdom or Old Empire; The First Intermediate Period; The Middle Kingdom or Middle Empire; The Second Intermediate Period; The New Kingdom or New Empire (1,532-1,070 B.C.E.); The third Intermediate Period (1,070-712 B.C.E.); The Late Period (712-332 B.C.E.).

In the Late Period the following groups controlled Egypt. The Nubian Dynasty (712-657 B.C.E.); The Persian Dynasty (525-404 B.C.E.); The Native Revolt and re-establishment of Egyptian rule by Egyptians (404-343 B.C.E.); The Second Persian Period (343-332 B.C.E.); The Ptolemaic or Greek Period (332 B.C.E.- c. 30 B.C.E.); Roman Period (c.30 B.C.E.-395 A.C.E.); The Byzantine Period (395-640 A.C.E) and The Arab Conquest Period (640 A.C.E.-present). The individual dynasties are numbered, generally in Roman numerals, from I through XXX. However, the realization of the geological evidence of the Great Sphinx and the discovery of the new Dynasty previously unknown to the Egyptologists, the history needs to be revised. See the full revision in the book African Origins of Civilization by Muata Ashby (2002).

The period after the New Kingdom saw greatness in culture and architecture under the rulership of Ramses II. However, after his rule, Egypt saw a decline from which it would never recover. This is the period of the downfall of Ancient Egyptian culture in which the Libyans ruled after the Tanite (XXI) Dynasty. This was followed by the Nubian conquerors who founded the XXII Dynasty and tried to restore Egypt to her past glory. However, having been weakened by the social and political turmoil of wars, Ancient Egypt fell to the Persians once more. The Persians conquered the country until the Greeks, under Alexander, conquered them. The Romans followed the Greeks, and finally the Arabs conquered the land of Egypt in 640 A.C.E to the present.

However, the history which has been classified above is only the history of the "Dynastic Period." It reflects the view of traditional Egyptologists who have refused to accept the evidence of a Predynastic period in Ancient Egyptian history contained in Ancient Egyptian documents such as the *Palermo Stone, Royal Tablets at Abydos, Royal Papyrus of Turin,* the *Dynastic List* of *Manetho,* and the eye-witness accounts of Greek historians Herodotus (c. 484-425 B.C.E.) and Diodorus. These sources speak clearly of a Pre-dynastic society which stretches far into antiquity. The Dynastic Period is what most people think of whenever Ancient Egypt is mentioned. This period is when the pharaohs (kings) ruled. The latter part of the Dynastic Period is when the Biblical story of Moses, Joseph, Abraham, etc., occurs (c. 2100? -1,000? B.C.E). Therefore, those with a Christian background generally only have an idea about Ancient Egypt as it is related in the Bible. The tradition based on the old Jewish bible recounting about how the Jews were used for forced labor and the construction of the great monuments of Egypt such as the Great Pyramids is impossible since these were created in the predynastic age, thousands of years before Abraham, the supposed first Jew, ever existed. Although this biblical notion is very limited in scope, the significant impact of Ancient Egypt on Hebrew and Christian culture is evident even from the biblical scriptures. Actually, Egypt existed much earlier than most traditional Egyptologists are prepared to admit. The new archeological evidence related to the great Sphinx monument on the Giza Plateau and the ancient writings by Manetho, one of the last High Priests of Ancient Egypt, show that Ancient Egyptian history begins earlier than 10,000 B.C.E. and may date back to as early as 30,000-50,000 B.C.E.

The Early History of Buddhism and the Egyptian Connection

An overview of the origins and development of Buddhism will provide further insights into its relationship with Africa and Ancient Egypt. The historical Buddha, Siddhartha Gautama (c. 563- c. 483 B.C.E.) was mythically related to have been a prince who gave up his royal life to seek after spiritual evolution. The traditional story of this life relates that he turned to the Brahmins, the Hindu Monks, and practiced austerities, but felt that he was obtaining minimal results from his efforts. The myth goes on to say that he then turned inwards and discovered a new path to attain spiritual salvation. It was called the middle way. He developed the Eight-Fold Path. A brief look at Buddhist history reveals that Buddhism developed in a similar way as Orthodox Christianity.

Right after the death of Buddha, his followers met for the first time to decide how to best preserve the teachings of the Buddha since they were never written down. When asked about who would lead the Buddhist faith, Buddha had told them they should work out their enlightenment on their own. However, the oral nature of the teachings made them subject to variation and misinterpretation. His disciples felt the need to convene a council to decide on what the "cannon" of the teachings would be. Hundreds of years later the Roman Christians held similar councils to decide on what Jesus had said and taught since nothing was written about him during the time he had supposedly lived. There were four major councils, in total, that convened to decide on the Buddhist teachings in its early development.

One hundred years later (c. 383 B.C.E.) , a second great council met at Vaishâli. In the 3rd century B.C.E., the third council was called by King Ashoka at Pâtaliputra (present-day Patna). Its purpose was to purify the *sangha* (membership) due to the large number of charlatans (false monks and heretics) who became Buddhists since it had attained royal patronage. The compilation of the Buddhist scriptures (Tipitaka) was supposed to have been completed at this time and also *abhidharma,* an adjunct philosophy to the Dharma doctrine was added along with the set monastic discipline (vinaya) that monks had recited at the first council. After this council, missionaries were sent to various countries. It is at this time that there is firm evidence of the Buddhist presence in Memphis, Egypt. This association continued for the next three centuries until the closing of the Egyptian Temples. However, there was still contact between Egypt and the Buddhists into the early Christian era, up to and after the fourth council of Buddhism. The fourth council was held about 100 A.C.E. The main goal of this council was to make peace between the sects. However, the Theravada Buddhists did not recognize authenticity of this council. So the teachings of Buddhism were not committed to writing until about the 1st century B.C.E., some 650 years after Buddha had lived.

Conflicting interpretations of the Buddhist teaching led to the development of no less than 18 schools of Buddhist philosophy. Out of these 18 or more sects of early Buddhism only the Theravada survives. All others that we see in the world today developed later in history. The more conservative monks were accused of not taking into account the needs of the general populace and so a new sect was created to serve the needs of the laity. That new sect was called Mahayana. It developed also out of conflicting Buddhist tenets. The conservative Theravadas viewed Buddha as a perfectly enlightened human teacher.

However, the liberal Mahasanghikas created a concept of Buddha an omnipresent, eternal, transcendental being. They thought that the human Buddha was only a manifestation of the transcendental Buddha that was sent to the earth for the good of humankind. In this conceptualization of Buddha nature, the Mahasanghika concept was a forerunner of Mahayana Buddhism (Buddhism for the masses). Mahayana Buddhists do not limit themselves to the original teachings of the Buddha nor to a canon of Buddhist writings. Their origins, as a group with a differing interpretation of Buddhist philosophy, are not known and yet they form a major aspect of modern Buddhism, the development of which is believed to have begun sometime between the 2nd century B.C.E. and the 1st century A.C.E.

Egyptian God in the Buddhist Pantheon

The contact of early Buddhism with Ancient Egypt has been verified during the period of king Ashoka, in the city of Menefer (Memphis). However, the contact continued and was later verified that there were Buddhists in the Ancient Egyptian city of Alexandria. There a special form of Buddhism developed that spread throughout Asia Minor (Middle East) between 100 B.C.E and 200 A.C.E. In the 2nd century ACE, the Christian dogmatist Clement of Alexandria[17] (pictured at here) recognized the Ancient Egyptian priests and priestesses and Bactrian Buddhists (Sramanas) for their influence on Greek thought:

> "Thus philosophy, a thing of the highest utility, flourished in antiquity among the barbarians, shedding its light over the

nations. And afterwards it came to Greece. First in its ranks were the prophets of the Egyptians;[18] and the Chaldeans among the Assyrians; and the Druids among the Gauls; and the Sramanas among the Bactrians ("Σαρμαναίοι Βάκτρων"); and the philosophers of the Celts; and the Magi of the Persians, who foretold the Saviour's birth, and came into the land of Judaea guided by a star. The Indian gymnosophists are also in the number, and the other barbarian philosophers. And of these there are two classes, some of them called Sramanas ("Σαρμάναι"), and others Brahmins ("Βραφμαναι")." Clement of Alexandria "The Stromata, or Miscellanies" Book I, Chapter XV[21].

The very first images of Buddha came about due to the association of the early Buddhists with the culture of the Greeks under Alexander who had conquered Egypt and India. Those images developed into a syncretic form of art that melded Greek and Buddhist conceptions. That period of Buddhist development in the area that is today known as Pakistan and the Indus as well as Persia (Iran) and in Alexandria Egypt, is referred to as Greco-Buddhism. However, the Greek conceptions were not wholly Greek. They had been "Egyptianized." One example of the influence of Ancient Egyptian influence can be seen in the images that incorporate an Ancient Egyptian God. The Ancient Egyptian influence reached as far as Japanese Buddhism.

Several other Buddhist deities may have been influenced by Greek gods. For example, Heracles with a lion-skin (who also happens to be the protector deity of Demetrius I) "served as an artistic model for Vajrapani, a protector of the Buddha" (Foltz, "Religions and the Silk Road") (See 1-

http://www.exoticindiaart.com/artimages/Bu
ddhaImage/greece_sm.jpg and 2-
http://faculty.maxwell.syr.edu/gaddis/HST2
10/Oct21/Heracles-Vajrapani.jpg). In Japan,
this expression further translated into the
wrath-filled and muscular Niō guardian gods
of the Buddha, standing today at the
entrance of many Buddhist temples.[19]

1   2

Vajrapani(Sanskrit   *Vajra*:thunderbolt/diamond,
Pani:lit.in the hand) is one of the earliest bodhisattvas
of Mahayana Buddhism. He is the protector and
guide of the Buddha, and rose to symbolize the
Buddha's power.
Vayrapani was used extensively in Buddhist
iconography as one of the three protective deities
surrounding the Buddha. Each of them symbolizes
one of the Buddha's virtues: Manjusri (the
manifestation of all the Buddhas' wisdom),
Avalokitesvara (the manifestation of all the Buddhas'

compassion) and Vajrapani (the manifestation of all the Buddhas' power).

Iconography

The first representations of Vajrapani in India associated him with the Hindu God Indra. As Buddhism expanded in Central Asia, and fused with Hellenistic influences into Greco-Buddhism, the Greek god Hercules was adopted to represent Vajrapani. He was then typically depicted as a hairy, muscular athlete, wielding a short "diamond" club.

Mahayana Buddhism then further spread to China, Korea and Japan from the 6th century.

In Japan, Vajrapani is known as Shukongōshin (執金剛神, "Diamond rod-wielding God"), and has

been the inspiration for the Niō (仁王, lit. Benevolent kings),the wrath-filled and muscular guardian god of the Buddha, standing today at the entrance of many Buddhist temples under the appearance of frightening wrestler-like statues.[20]

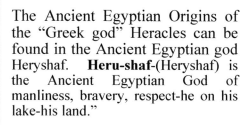

The Ancient Egyptian Origins of the "Greek god" Heracles can be found in the Ancient Egyptian god Heryshaf. **Heru-shaf**-(Heryshaf) is the Ancient Egyptian God of manliness, bravery, respect-he on his lake-his land."

He is recognized as a form of Heru, as his name denotes, since it contains the *Her* spelling (spelling of the name of Heru when written fully -Heru), he was later identified by the Greeks with the Greek Heracles (Hercules) and the Ancient Egyptian town he came from was called Herakleopolis "town of Heracles." He is known in Neterian myth as the "Ba Asar" and "Ba Ra" or soul of Asar and soul of Ra. He wears the Atef (Crown of Asar).

$$\text{𓅃}\bigcirc\text{𓏭}\text{𓃾}\text{ or }\text{𓃾}\text{𓅆}\text{𓏭}\text{𓃾}\quad Meril$$

The Nubian divinity Meril is referred to as the "beloved lion" divinity of the city of Kalabshah (city located 35 miles south of the modern Egyptian city Aswan), where the temple of Khnum is located. In ancient times it was known as Abu (Greek Elephantine) by the Greeks or the first cataract of Egypt. Today it is called Aswan. Meril, a Ram-headed divinity like the Heru aspect Hery-shaf (Heryshaf), was recognized as a manifestation of Heru and Ra. He is regarded as the sun-god of northern Nubia. The Greeks identified him with Apollo and Heracles.

The ancient Greeks themselves admit that they adopted the Ancient Egyptian gods and goddesses as their own. In short, what is regarded as Greek was in reality a patchwork of differing ideas which had their basis in Ancient Egyptian philosophy, but which did not follow its precepts entirely. The following passages from the writings of Herodotus (*The Histories*) are instructive on the Ancient Egyptian origins of the Greek gods and goddesses *(highlighted portions are by Ashby)*.

> 35. **"Almost all the names of the gods came into Greece from Egypt. My inquiries prove that they were all derived from a foreign source, and my opinion is that Egypt furnished the greater number**. For with the exception of Neptune and the Dioscuri, whom I mentioned above, and Juno, Vesta, Themis, the Graces, and the Nereids, **the other gods have been known from time immemorial in Egypt**. This I assert on the authority of the Egyptians themselves."
> —Herodotus (c. 484-425 BC)

> "And upon his return to Greece, they gathered around and asked, "tell us about this great land of the Blacks called Ethiopia." And Herodotus said, "There are two great Ethiopian nations, one in Sind (India) and the other in Egypt."
> —Herodotus (c. 484-425 BC)

Before Alexander the Great of Greece, the Egyptians had conquered the land s of Asia Minor (Cannaan (Palestine), Ur (Iraq), Persia (Iran), Indus (Pakistan) and Sind (India).

> "There are Egyptian columns as far off as NYASA, Arabia...Isis and Osiris led an army into India, to the source of the Ganges, and as far as the Indus Ocean."

-*Diodorus* (Greek historian 100 B. C.)

> 38. "In early times the Pelasgi, as I know by information which I got at Dodona, offered sacrifices of all kinds, and prayed to the gods, but had no distinct names or appellations for them, since they had never heard of any. They called them gods, because they disposed and arranged all things in such a beautiful order. *After a long lapse of time the names of the gods came to Greece from Egypt,* and the Pelasgi learnt them, only as yet they knew nothing of Bacchus, of whom they first heard at a much later date."

We are informed by the Greeks themselves that they derived most of their gods and goddesses from Ancient Egypt, and we are also informed that their most important spiritual philosophers, who created Greek philosophy, studied in Egypt.

> "This is also confirmed by the most learned of Greeks such as Solon, Thales, Plato, Eudoxus, Pythagoras, and as some say, even Lycurgus going to Egypt and conversing with the priests; of whom they say Euxodus was a hearer of Chonuphis of

Memphis,[21] Solon of Sonchis of Sais,[22] and Pythagoras of Oenuphis of Heliopolis.[23]"
-Plutarch, Morals, 10
(c. 46-120 AD), Greek author/Initiate of Isis (Aset).

The statements of the ancient Romans who saw a continuous culture from Ethiopia to India corroborate the statements of the ancient Greeks.

"India taken as a whole, beginning from the north and embracing what of it is subject to Persia, is a continuation of Egypt and the Ethiopians."
-The Itinerarium Alexandri (A.C.E. 345)

Common Philosophical Concepts in Buddhism and Neterianism (Ancient Egyptian Religion)

The Concept of the Trinity in Buddhism

The Mahayana sect developed the doctrine of Buddha's threefold nature, or triple "body" (*trikaya*) - body of essence (ultimate nature), the body of communal bliss, and the body of transformation. Beyond the body of essence there is transcendence of form. There is the realm or state of consciousness which is changeless and absolute. This transcendental Absolute is also referred to as consciousness or the void. The essential Buddha nature manifests itself as communal bliss as well as takes on human form in order to assist human beings. Siddhartha Gautama was just one example of the body of transformation form of the historical Buddha. A similar debate as the one about the nature of Buddha raged on amongst the orthodox Christians about the nature of Jesus Christ.

The debates in the church over the true understanding of Christ (Christology) led to a separation between the Church in Egypt (Coptic Church) and the churches of Rome and Constantinople (Western Empire and Eastern Empire). The majority of Egyptian Christians refused to go along with the decrees of the Council of Chalcedon in 451 A.C.E., that defined the person of Jesus the Christ as being "one in two natures." This doctrine of "two natures" seemed to imply the existence of two Christs, one being divine and the other human. The Egyptian Christians who refused the Council of Chalcedon faced charges of monophysitism. Monophysitism is the belief that Christ has only one nature rather than two. It is notable that the Council of Chalcedon was accepted both in Constantinople and in Rome, but not in Egypt. Thus, we see that the dualistic view of Christ was developed and promoted in Europe under the Roman church and in the Middle East under the church of Constantinople. It was Egypt, which sought to uphold the non-dualistic view of Christ, which viewed him as an all-encompassing Divine being. This was due to the tradition of non-dualism, which it assimilated from the Ancient Egyptian mystery schools. The Coptic Church of Egypt separated from Rome and Constantinople and set up its own Pope who, to this day, is nominated by an Electoral College of clergy and laity. The Coptic Church has survived up to the present in Egypt. There are over seven million Coptic Christians there today and 22 million in total.

The Concept of The Trinity in Christianity

In the New Testament, the triad of "Father, and of the Son, and of the Holy Spirit" is used to describe the idea of God (Matthew 28:19). The Trinity is a central teaching of Christianity. It holds that God is three personalities, the Father, the Son, and the Holy Spirit [or Holy Ghost]. The idea is that there is only one God, but that he exists as *"Three."* Christian theologians claim that the true nature of the Trinity is a mystery, which cannot be comprehended by the human mind, although they can grasp some of its meanings. The Trinity doctrine was stated in very early Christian creeds whose purpose was to counter other beliefs such as Gnosticism. However, as we saw earlier, later church authorities misunderstood it.

The Concept of Trinity According to Ancient Egyptian Religion and Mystical Philosophy

The term *"Trinity"* was misunderstood by the Orthodox Catholic Christians and, because of this misunderstanding; some Gnostic groups even ridiculed them. However, the three in one metaphor was ancient by the time it was adopted by Catholicism. It was a term used to convey the idea of different aspects of the one reality. This same idea occurs in Egyptian as well as in Indian mythology.

However, for deeper insights into the mystical meaning of the Trinity we must look to Ancient Egyptian mysticism. In Egyptian mythology, the Trinity was represented as three *metaphysical neters* {neteru} or gods and goddesses. They represent the manifestation of the unseen principles, which support the universe, and the visible aspects of God. The main Egyptian Trinity is composed of *Amun, Ra and Ptah*. Amun means that which is hidden and unintelligible, the underlying reality which sustains all things. Ra represents the subtle matter of creation as well as the mind. Ptah represents the visible aspect of Divinity, the phenomenal universe. The Ancient Egyptian "Trinity" is also known as a manifestation of *Nebertcher* (Neberdjer). Nebertcher means "all encompassing" Divinity. Thus, the term is equivalent to the Vedantic Brahman, the Buddhist Dharmakaya and the Taoist Tao. The Ancient Egyptian text reads as follows:

"Everything is Amun-Ra-Ptah, three in one."

Each member of the Trinity had a particular city in Egypt where the mysticism of each individual divinity was espoused. In each city, each divinity had their own Trinity, of which each was the head. In the city of Memphis, where the early Buddhists lived and studied, the local Trinity was headed by the Ancient Egyptian divinity Ptah. This Trinity consisted of Ptah, Sekhmit and Nefertum. In this system, Ptah represents Consciousness manifesting as mind, Sekhmit represents Life Force and Nefertum represents Creation as well as enlightened consciousness. Also, Nefertum is the prince of Menefer {Memphis} and his father, Ptah, is the supreme preceptor of Memphite Theology. So this teaching of the Trinity at Memphis was studied by the early Buddhists and they were also impressed by the popular quality of Memphite Theology. While Memphite Theology is highly philosophical and intellectual, it is also personable because its teaching involves myths and deities to which people can relate. Also, the Ancient Egyptians were adept at conducting rituals that involved the entire population, thereby allowing them to take part in the mysteries of the religion, and at such time when they proved their readiness, individuals were admitted to the priestly ranks to worship and be privy to the higher teachings behind the myth.[24]

The Buddha or *"The Enlightened One"*,[25] developed a philosophy based on ideas which existed previously in Jain philosophy and the Upanishads as well as Ancient Egypt. Buddha recognized that many people took the teachings to extreme. Teachings such as that of non-violence which stressed not harming any creatures were understood by some as not moving so as not to step on insects or not breathing in without covering the mouth so as not to kill insects or microorganisms. Prior to Buddha, other teachings such as those of the "Brahmins" and "Sanyasa" (renunciates), where one was supposed to renounce the apparent reality as an illusion, were taken to extremes wherein some followers would starve themselves to the point of death in order to achieve spiritual experience. Others became deeply involved with the intellectual aspects of philosophy, endlessly questioning, "Where did I come from?, Who put me here?, How long will I need to do spiritual practice?, Where did Brahman (GOD) come from?", etc. Buddha saw the error of the way in which the teaching was understood and set out to reform religion.

Buddha emphasized attaining salvation rather than asking so many questions. He likened people who asked too many intellectual questions to a person whose house (lifetime) is burning down while they ask "How did the fire get started?" instead of first worrying about getting out. Further, Buddha saw that renouncing attachment to worldly objects was not necessarily a physical discipline but more importantly, it was a psychological one and therefore, he created a philosophical discipline which explained the psychology behind human suffering and how to end that suffering, a philosophy emphasizing "BALANCE" rather than extremes. He recognized that extremes cause mental upset-ness because *"One extreme leads to another."* Therefore, mental balance was the way to achieve mental peace. This psychological discipline became the Noble Eight-fold Path which was later adapted by the Indian Sage Patanjali and developed into the eight major Yoga disciplines of Indian Yoga. The concept of balance is reflected in the Ancient Egyptian Maat Philosophy, which requires aspirants to live in balance, refraining from extremes.

While never formally rejecting the existence of the gods and goddesses, Buddhism some sects deny any special role to them. These beings may have pleasurable and long lives in the heavens but they are under the same ultimate law as human beings and other creatures. They are not considered as creators and they must ultimately die and be reborn again. Buddhism does hold that they do not control the destiny of human beings and so there is no value in praying to them.

This same philosophy that the gods and goddesses are subject to the same ultimate law as are human beings and other creatures is reflected in the Anunian Theology based at the city of Anu, a short distance from Memphis. It held that God, in the form of Ra, the second member of the Great Trinity, emanates the gods and goddesses from himself and they constitute the elements of Creation. He periodically ("after millions and millions of years") dissolves the world back into himself including the gods and goddesses.[26] A similar teaching is contained in the Asarian Theology which is associated with Memphite Theology.[27] However, Ancient Egyptian religion, across the board, and African religion in general, hold that there is value in approaching the gods and goddesses. That lower form of worship promotes the ability to understand and approach the Supreme Being.

One important difference between Buddhism and the other Hindu religions is that Buddhism does not advocate worshipping Buddha, whereas most other Indian religions do incorporate the worshiping of a deity or other divine figure(s). However, Buddha is to be paid homage and to be emulated through the practice of Buddhist teaching. This practice leads the aspirant to discovering his/her own essential "Buddha Nature." So if a person is interested in a psychological spiritual discipline rather than a religious based system of deities, Buddhism offers less images of deities on the surface. However, many followers of the Buddhist religion develop a deep reverential devotion to the Buddha and, in essence, "deify" him. Also, the Mahayana form of Buddhism offers many "Buddhas" which can be equated to deities. They symbolize various aspects of consciousness and various aspects of Buddhist philosophy.

The Shabaka Inscription and the Mythology of Memphite Theology

Above- The Shabaka Stone (now with much of its text rubbed off due to mishandling)

The Shabaka Inscription contains the mythological and philosophical basis of Memphite Theology. It contains a rendition of the Creation Myth of Memphite Theology which explains the origins of Ptah and how Creation came into being. The nature and composition of *"matter,"* or what is termed *"physical reality,"* and the concept of *"consciousness"* were understood and clearly set down in the hieroglyphic texts which date back to 5000 B.C.E in the theological system of Memphis, Egypt, as follows:

1. *"Ptah conceived in his heart* (reasoning consciousness-mind) all that would exist and at his utterance (the word - will, power to make manifest), created Nun, the primeval waters (unformed matter-energy).

2. Then not having a place to sit Ptah causes Nun to emerge from the primeval waters as the Primeval Hill so that he may have a place to sit. Atom then emerges and sits upon Ptah. Then came out of the

waters four pairs of gods and goddesses, the Ogdoad (eight Gods):

3. Nun (primeval waters) and Nunet (heaven).
4. Huh (boundlessness) and Huhet (that which has boundaries).
5. Kuk (darkness) and Kuket (light).
6. Amon (the hidden) and Amonet (that which is manifest).

7. *The Neteru (Nun, Nunet, Huh, Huhet, Kuk, Kuket, Amon, Amonet) are the lips and teeth of (God's) mouth which speaks the names of all things which come into existence . . .*

8. *. . The Heart and tongue have power over all the limbs. God is found as the heart within all bodies, and in the mouth of each neter and all humans as the tongue (will), of all things that live. . . It is God who thinks (as the Heart) and who commands (as the tongue). . .*

9. . . . That which the nose breathes, the eyes see, the ears hear; all of these (senses) are communicated to the heart. *It is the heart (mind) which makes all knowledge and awareness manifest, and then the tongue is what repeats what the heart has thought. .*
.

10. . . . All divine utterances manifested themselves through the thoughts of the heart and the commandments of the tongue. . .

11. . . . Justice is done to they who do what is loved, punishment to they who do what is hated. Life is given to they who are peaceful, death is given to the criminal. . .

12. . . .In truth God (Ptah) caused the neteru to be born, the creation of the cities, establishment of the

nomes, the establishment of the neteru in their places of adoration. . . God made their likenesses according to their desire. Thereby, the neteru entered into their bodies, the variety of wood, all types of mineral, clay, and all things that grow from these and in which they have taken place, foods, provisions, and all good things... He (Ptah) is Heru."

13. Thus is it to be understood that Ptah is the mightiest of all Divinities.

Through the Shabaka Inscription we are to understand that Ptah created the gods and goddesses (Verse 3) through his *thought and desire* i.e. will, (verse 1-2) and they became the manifested creation which is like the body that the gods and goddesses, i.e. the spirit, exists in. In essence, since God is the innermost reality within *"each neter"* (god or goddess) and *"all humans,"* it is actually God who is thinking, perceiving and experiencing through them (Verse 5). Further, it is God who not only made the objects of creation (*the variety of wood, all types of mineral, clay, and all things that grow from these and in which they have taken place, foods, provisions, and all good things...*), but it is actually God (Ptah) who is in the objects of Creation and Creation is his body (Verse 9). In this manner, as in Buddhism, the mystic practitioner is to realize the mental nature of the universe. The mind and consequently psychology, is the key to understanding the universe and consequently also understanding God as well. The mind controls the tongue (sound-vibration – verse 7) and by righteousness (verse 8) an initiate can come to discern the mental act or will which has brought forth and sustains Creation. These are fundamental Buddhist concepts:

1. Suffering due to vices vs. peace and righteousness, Maat, which includes Truth: Maat is Right Action, Non-violence, Right Action- self-control, Right

Speech, Right Worship, Selfless Service, Balance of Mind - Reason – Right Thinking, Not-stealing, Sex-Sublimation, and Maat Offering (uniting with the Divinity).

2. Creation and enlightenment by mental act,
3. Right Understanding, Ptah is the supreme Being and all objects in Creation proceed from him and are constructs of his mind.
4. Ptah "gave birth" to the gods and goddesses as the Buddhist "Dharmakaya," the cosmic father-mother gave birth to the cosmos.

Ancient Egyptian Memphite Theology, Indian Vaishnavism and Indian Buddhism

Buddhism was a movement to counter what was seen by Buddhists as over-dependence on ritual and faith-based religious practice without substantive psychological and inner transformative development that much of Hinduism had degraded to at the time. While Shetaut Neter, Ancient Egyptian religion, did have important areas of correlation with Hindu traditions such as Vaishnavism and Buddhism, because of the connection between Ancient Egypt and India in Ancient times, that should not be taken to mean that the Vaishnavites or Buddhists later practiced the same exact teachings and disciplines as the Ancient Egyptians; there were changes. Yet, the correlations provide insight into the philosophical relationships between Shetaut Neter and Hinduism as well as between Shetaut Neter and Buddhism.

Vaishnavism is the worship of the divinity Vishnu and his incarnations. As explained earlier, Vishnu is a Vedic divinity that was adopted into the Early Hindu tradition of India albeit in a transformed way. His attributes were elevated above those of Indra, the king of the Vedic divinities and his incarnations were the subjects of the important Hindu epics, Ramayana and Mahabharata. The following comparison between the myth of Memphis in Ancient Egypt and the Vaishnava tradition of ancient India provides insight into the affinity of the Indians for this Ancient Egyptian tradition (Memphite Theology), to the extent of founding a settlement in Menefer (Hetkaptah - Memphis). It also gives insight into the philosophy of Memphite Theology that also appealed to the Buddhists from India who also came there. The Indian teachings of Vishnu, the Lotus, the Cosmic Serpent, The Creator

Divinity sitting on the Lotus which arises out of the Primeval Ocean, etc., occur in the Ancient Egyptian Anunian-Memphite Theology. The Creator Divinity, the principle called "Brahma" in Indian myth is called "Khepri" or "Nefertum" in Ancient Egyptian myth.

Above- The Ancient Egyptian *Ptah-Tanen (Tem)* sitting on the primeval ocean with the sundisk (Tem, Nefertum) issuing from his head, his seat has the Sema (Sma) symbol of mystic union.

Ptah, Nefertum and the Mysticism of the Memphite Trinity

The Egyptian Trinity mythology of *Amun-Ra-Ptah* represents a major philosophical discourse on the composition of nature and the path of Kamitan spirituality. Memphite Theology, based on the god Ptah, is only a third of the entire teaching. Ptah is the Supreme Spirit and he manifests Creation through his consort Sekhmit and their child Nefertum. The Trinity of Memphis (Ptah-Sekhmit-Nefertum) relates to a profound understanding of the nature of Creation. Ptah is the hidden inner essence of creation and the essence of the human soul as well. Like Vishnu, in Hindu myth, Ptah is passive, immobile and detached. He "thinks" Creation into being by his will and has indeed become the Universe, through the actions of the Creator Nefertum. Ptah's thoughts are transformed into "word" (i.e. vibrations), and these cause the Nun (primeval Ocean) to take the varied forms of Creation which are described in detail in the foremost scripture of Memphite Theology, the "Shabaka Stone Inscription."[28] This philosophy means that just as wind and its motion are one and the same, and the ocean and its waves are one and the same, in the same way, the Supreme Self and the objects of the world are one and the same. According to Memphite Theology, the world is composed of *neteru*. These neterus are divine energy, cosmic forces that constitute all physical phenomena. These neteru have assumed the bodies (forms) of all the objects in the world which appear on the surface to be different and separate from each other, but in reality, the neteru are essentially conditioned aspects of God and therefore God has entered into all forms of existence.

Memphite Theology is actually a unique form of the Kamitan religion in that it is highly philosophical and oriented towards intellectual development leading towards intuitional realization of the nature of Self. In this sense it is no surprise to find that the early Buddhists and Hindus (Upanishadic-Vedantic tradition), which were disciplines emphasizing psychology and philosophy, developed an affinity for the city of Memphis and became attached to its temple which promoted the teachings of Memphite Theology, since they all have much in common with the Buddhist and Hindu teachings. The Memphite scripture elucidates on the process of Creation and in its fundamental principles it is strikingly parallel with those of Hinduism. Ptah thinks and a Creator, Tem, on his lotus, comes into existence and Creation is brought forth.

> "2- Then, not having a place to sit Ptah
> causes Nun to emerge from the primeval

waters as the Primeval Hill so that he may
have a place to sit. Atom then emerges and
sits upon Ptah."[29]

In order to understand and appreciate the word
Nefertum and its relation to the Indian Brahma more fully,
its definition and function will now be presented. Nefertum
means "beautiful completion." In the Ancient Egyptian
Book of Coming Forth By Day it is said that when an
initiate attains resurrection, i.e. Spiritual enlightenment,
they are actually becoming Nefertum. In the Creation Myth
of the city of Anu (Anunian Theology), Tem is the divine
aspect of the spirit as the first individuated entity to emerge
from the primeval ocean. Also, in a separate but related
teaching, from the myth of Ra and Aset, Tem is referred to
as the third aspects of Ra as follows.

In the myth of Ra and Aset, Ra says: *"I am Kheperi in
the morning, and Ra at noonday, and Temu in the
evening."* Thus we have *Kheper-Ra-Tem,* ⊙◠ⲯ仒⏋, as the
Anunian Triad. In Chapter 4 of the *Prt m Hru,* the initiate
identifies {him/her} self with Tem, symbolizing that
{his/her} life as a human being with human consciousness
is coming to an end. Instead of an awareness of
individuality and human limitation, there is now a new
awareness of infinity and immortality, even though the
physical body continues to exist and will die in the normal
course of time. The initiate will live on as a "living" soul
and join with Tem (individual consciousness joins Cosmic
Consciousness):

"I am Tem in rising; I am the only One; I
came into being with Nu. I am Ra who rose
in the beginning."

Figure: The Ancient Egyptian divinity: Nefertum

The passage above is very important because it establishes the mystical transcendence of the initiate who has realized {his/her} "oneness" and union with the Divine. In other Ancient Egyptian papyri, Tem is also identified with the young Herupakhart (Harmachis -young Heru, the solar child) as the early morning sun. Thus, Kheperi-Ra-Temu are forms of the same being and are the object of every initiate's spiritual goal. Being the oldest of the three theologies, the Mysteries of Anu (Anunian Theology) formed a foundation for the unfolding of the teachings of mystical spirituality which followed in the mysteries of Hetkaptah (Memphis- Memphite Theology), through Ptah, and the Mysteries of Waset (Thebes- Theban Theology), through Amun. With each succeeding exposition, the teaching becomes more and more refined until it reaches its quintessence in the Hymns of Amun.

In the Ancient Egyptian Pyramid Texts there is a very important passage which provides insight into the role of Nefertum and the entire teaching behind the Trinity of Memphite Theology.

> "I become Nefertum, the lotus-bloom which is at the nostril of Ra; I will come forth from the horizon every day and the gods and goddesses will be cleansed at the sight of me."
>
> —Ancient Egyptian Pyramid Texts

Thus, we are to understand that Ptah is the source, the substratum from which all creation arises. Ptah is the will of the Spirit, giving rise to thought itself and that thought takes form as Sekhmit, Creation itself. The same spirit, Ptah, who enlivens Creation, is the very essence which rises above Creation to complete the cycle of Spirit to matter and then back to Spirit. The Lotus is the quintessential symbol of completion, perfection and glory. Thus it is used in Ancient Egyptian and Hindu mythologies as the icon par excellence of spiritual enlightenment. Therefore, smelling the lotus, and acting as the lotus means moving above the muddy waters of Creation and turning towards the sun which is the symbol of Ra, the Supreme Spirit.

In Chapter 24 of the *Pert M Heru (Book of Coming Forth By Day)*, the role of goddess Hetheru in the process of salvation is specified as the initiate speaks the words which will help {him/her} become as a lotus:

> "I am the lotus, pure, coming forth out into the day. I am the guardian of the nostril of Ra and keeper of the nose of Hetheru. I

make, I come, and I seek after he, that is
Heru. I am pure going out from the field."

Both the lotus and the sun have been used since ancient
times to symbolize the detachment and dispassion that a
spiritual aspirant must develop towards the world, that is,
turning away from relating to the world from the perception
of the limited senses and the conditioned mind, and rather,
turning towards the underlying reality and sustainer of
Creation, the illuminating transcendental Spirit, as
symbolized by the sun. The lotus is a solar symbol, and as
such is a wonderful metaphor for the process of spiritual
evolution leading to Enlightenment. The lotus emerges
everyday out of the murky waters of the pond in order to
receive the rays of the sun. As it rises up through the murky
waters to rise above, its leaves, which have a special
coating or texture, promotes the water to run right off of
them without a drop sticking or clinging to them. It then
opens and blooms to the light of the sun. The spiritual
aspirant, a follower of the Goddess, seeking to experience
the Supreme Spirit, must rise {him/her} self up through the
murky waters of egoism and negativity (anger, hatred,
greed, and ignorance), eventually to rise above, leaving all
remnants behind (i.e. transcending them), as {he/she}
blooms to the light of the Self, i.e. attain Enlightenment.
Hetheru and Heru form a composite archetype, a savior
with all of the complementary qualities of the male and
female principles, inseparable, complete and androgynous.

Table: The Fundamental Principles of Memphite Theology and Vaishnavism

Ancient Egyptian Memphite Theology	✓	Hindu Vaishnavism	Mythological and Philosophical Principles
NUN	⇔	NARA	The primeval Ocean, Nun and Nara, in both Ancient Egyptian and Indian myth, respectively, refer to the ocean of potential consciousness which can assume any form, i.e. the objects of Creation. It is this ocean which transforms itself into the objects and living beings of the universe. This ocean is the body, as it were, of the Divine (God, the Spirit).
PTAH-SOKAR	⇔	VISHNU	Both divinities, Ptah and Vishnu, hold the same mythological position. They are the "immovable" or "actionless" undivided Spirit, who emerges from the primeval ocean (Nun – Nara) and engenders a creative principle to do the work of creation. They symbolize the principle of pure individuality, the first "I am." Arising from the ocean of pure consciousness they will the "thought" of Creation. Ptah and Vishnu do not move. The creative principle performs all the action of creation and is sustained by the ocean of potential.
	⇔		
NEFERTEM		BRAHMA	That dynamic aspects (Nefertum – Brahma) of the individuated Spirit, the oneness, which emerge out of that first essence symbolize the principle of multiplicity, the force to produce many. From this one come the many differentiated forms of Creation. The Creator divinity arises out of the will of the Spirit.
	⇔		
NETERU		DEVA	The Creator brings forth creation by emanating creative energy (Neteru – Deva) or mythologically speaking, gods and goddesses, out of itself into the ocean of undifferentiated

			consciousness. Thereby, that part of the ocean that is moved by the creative energy assumes a particular form and quality. Thus, through the creator and the vibrations in the ocean of potential consciousness which are all aspects of the same Transcendental absolute, the Spirit transforms itself into the varied forms of Creation.

Correlations Between the Mystic Teachings of the Ancient Egyptian Coffin Texts and the Ancient Indian Upanishads

Findings from the discipline of Paleo-anthropology show a connection between Ancient Egypt and Ancient India. The specific evidence links the Ancient Egyptian peoples of Sakkara-Memphis with the Indus Valley Civilization (4,000 B.C.E.-3,000 B.C.E.).[30] Also, it was reported that an Indian colony existed in the city of Memphis at around 500 B.C.E.[31] Also there is documentation of the presence of Buddhist practitioners in Memphis. The deeper aspect of the mythic formats presented above, from Ancient Egypt and India, contain vast and profound schemes of cosmological and mystical teaching. The teachings of Memphite Theology, contained in the Shabaka Inscription and the attendant prayers and Hymns to Ptah are essentially a mythological interpretation of the Ancient Egyptian *Pert M Hru* or *Book of Enlightenment* texts (*Pyramid Texts, Coffin Texts and Papyrus Texts*). The myths of Hinduism are interpretations of the spiritual philosophy contained in the Upanishads, followed by the important Hindu epics (Mahabharata and the Ramayana). It is important to understand that the Upanishadic era literature is concerned with high philosophy and the gods and goddesses therefore assume a secondary role. The Later Classical epics called the

71

Puranas, which began appearing during the Gupta period (319-415 A.C.E.)[32] became the main source of modern Hindu mythology. By the 10th century A.C.E. the Puranas became the scriptures of the common man. Containing a great variety of legendary material, their main purpose, like all mythic scriptures such as the Asarian Resurrection of Egypt, the Gospels of Christianity, etc., was glorifying the gods and goddesses and not to prove historical events. In the case of Hinduism, the Puranas glorified Vishnu, Shiva, and Brahma for the purpose of engendering followers to the tradition, and not necessarily to provide a historical documentation. Of the eighteen principal Puranas that survive, the most popular is the Bhagavata-Purana on the early life of Krishna.[33] Therefore, it will be fruitful to compare the philosophical scriptures of Ancient Egypt and India. In doing so there are several important correlations between Ancient Egyptian and Indian spirituality.

> "After the millions of years of differentiated creation, the chaos that existed before creation will return; only the primeval god[i] and Asar will remain steadfast-no longer separated in space and time."
>
> –Ancient Egyptian *Coffin Texts*

The passage above concisely expresses the powerful teaching that all creation is perishable and that even the gods and goddesses will ultimately dissolve into the primordial state of potential consciousness. Therefore, it behooves a human being to move towards the Divine since that is the only stable truth that exists as an abiding reality. This is known as the Absolute, from which all has emanated and into which all will dissolve. *Tm* (Tem, Tum, Atum, Atum-Ra) is the Absolute, from which Creation

---

[i] Referring to the Supreme Being in the form of Atum-Ra

arises and into which Creation will dissolve. The same transcendental and non-dualist philosophy evident in the passage above from the *Coffin Texts* can be found in the Indian *Upanishads*.

> "Before creation came into existence, Brahman (the Absolute) existed as the Unmanifest. From the Unmanifest was created the manifest. From himself he brought forth himself. Hence he is known as the Self-Existent."
>
> —Taittiriya Upanishad

The Ancient Egyptian concept of Nun is powerfully expressed in the following passage from the *Coffin Texts.*

> "I am Nu, The Only One, without equal and I came into being at the time of my flood...I originated in the primeval void. I brought my body into existence through my own potency. I made myself and formed myself in accordance with my own desire. That which emanated from me was under my control."
>
> –Ancient Egyptian *Coffin Texts*

Once again, the initiate is to discover that the Divine Self is the substratum of manifest creation and that {his/her} deeper essence and the deeper essence of all humanity is that same Self-existent Divinity which brought the entire creation into being by the power of her own will and desire. Nun is an aspect of Tem. In this aspect, it is to be understood as a formless potential matter which can convert itself into any form and any element (earth, water, fire, metal, etc.). This process may be likened to how temperature affects water. For example, very cold water becomes ice, and ice can have any shape. When very hot, the water evaporates and becomes so subtle (vapor) as to be "unmanifest." At room temperature, he same water is visible but formless. All matter is like the water. All matter is composed of the same essence which takes on the form of various objects, just as clay can take many forms. However, the forms are not abiding but temporary. God has assumed the forms of Creation just as an actor assumes a part in a play. When the play is over, the actor's mask is stripped away and the true essence of the actor's identity is revealed, just as ice melts to reveal water. The Divine Self is the substratum of all that is manifest. The same philosophy, and using almost the same exact language, is evident in the Indian *Upanishads.*

> "...In the beginning there was Existence alone—One only, without a second. He, the One, thought to himself: Let me be many, let me grow forth. Thus, out of himself he projected the universe; and having projected the universe out of himself he entered into every being."
>
> —Chandogya Upanishad

This conceptualization in the Chandogya Upanishad (c.800 B.C.E.) which states that *"out of himself he projected the universe; and having projected the universe out of himself he entered into every being,"* is exactly the same conceptualization already present in the Memphite Theology (c.5000-3000 B.C.E.). Also, the highly intellectual and philosophical nature of Memphite Theology and its consequent similarity to Buddhism become evident. Thus, in the capacities outlined above, Memphite Theology is a compatible with Buddhism and the Upanishadic tradition.

Evidence of Contact Between Early Buddhists and Ancient Egyptians

Table: Timeline of Buddhism and Ancient Egypt

Time-line of Early Buddhism and Ancient Egypt

10,000 B.C.E	5000 B.C.E.	4500 B.C.E.	4000 B.C.E.	3500 B.C.E.	3000 B.C.E.	1500 B.C.E	1000 B.C.E.	500 B.C.E.	400 B.C.E.	250 B.C.E.	0	100 A.C.E.	300 A.C.E.
Ancient Egyptian Religion								Cambyses Invades Egypt Persian Period	Alexander Invades Egypt Greek Period				Coptic Period to Present
Pre-Dynastic Era	Old Kingdom		Middle Kingdom			New Kingdom							
			Indus Valley Culture			Aryan India		Hinduism in India to present					
								Council #1	Council #2	Council #3		Council #4	
						Buddhist Councils					Early Christianity	Pre-Roman	Orthodox Councils

General Timeline of Phases in Buddhist and Hindu Indian Myth and Religion

3000 – 1500 B.C.E. Indus Valley Period

1500 - 1000 B.C.E. Aryan Period

1000 - 800 B.C.E. Brahmanas period

800 – 600 Upanishadic Period

600 B.C.E.- 261 B.C.E. Early Hindu Period

500 B.C.E. Buddhism founded

261 B.C.E.- 1200 A.C.E. Buddhist prominence among conglomeration of other Indian belief systems.

319-415 A.C.E. Gupta period – Dynasty of Rulers of Magadha[34] Renaissance of Hinduism – Puranic Age

Between the years 319 A.C.E. to 1100 A.C.E., Hinduism experienced a resurgence and Buddhism began to wane in India. The older traditions of the Brahmins, Vedic students, as well as newer traditions, including Tantrism, Kundalini Yoga and several schools of Hindu mysticism emerged including Vedanta, Jainism,[35] Shaivism,[36] Vaishnavism,[37] Shaktism,[38] Tantrism,[39] Yoga,[40] Samkhya,[41] and others.[42] The Puranas, stories about glories of the Divine in human form on earth, were a rekindling force that caused people to take a new interest in Hindu myth, legend and spirituality. Much like the Christian gospels, their function was to engender a devotional feeling and to make the divinities, especially Krishna, personal as opposed to the monastic concept of Buddha which many people saw as being more rigid, intellectual and psychological. By 1,200 A.C.E. a Muslim Dynasty had come to power in India, and Buddhism virtually disappeared from the land of its origin. Many Buddhist elements still survive in Indian Hinduism.[43]

Some scholars believe that Buddhism waned in India not just because of the Muslim conquest, but also because in its purest form, Buddhism holds a view of God as consciousness as opposed to a supernatural figure (male or female) or spirit with a name and form. Some Hindus, such as the orthodox followers of Krishna[44] consider the Buddhists and Vedantins as "impersonalists" because they revere the Divine "without name and form" and see this as an incorrect practice of religion. The Muslims on the other hand, see Buddhists as "Kaffirs" or unbelievers because they do not follow Islam and because of this, according to them, they are not following religion at all. A stark example of the enmity between Buddhism and Islam was the extremist actions by some Muslims of destroying ancient Buddhist monuments in Afghanistan in the mid 1990's A.C.E.

Cultural-religious exchange between Egypt and India in the time of Emperor Ashoka in 261 B.C.E.

In the book *India and Egypt: Influences and Interactions, 1993,* Lutfi A. W. Yehya notes the archeological discoveries, in Ancient Egypt of the Ptolemaic era, which conclusively prove contact between the Ancient Egyptians and Indians of that time as well as a blending of Ancient Egyptian and Indian religion as evinced by the artifacts found in Memphis, Egypt.

> "There seems to be sufficient evidence to indicate that Indians in good number had started visiting Egypt in the Ptolemaic period and even before it-from the third century, BC onwards. Athenaeus refers to the presence of Indian women, Indian cows and camels, and Indian hunting dogs in the royal processions of Ptolemy Philadelphus in Egypt.[45] An Indian colony probably existed in Egypt even earlier at Memphis. The excavations at Memphis have yielded some terracotta fragments and figurines[46] which from their facial features and costume, appear to be Indian.[47] Some of

them have been identified as the representations of Panchika, a Buddhist divinity.[48]

Again, indicative of the close contact during

Ptolemaic times is a gravestone which bears an Indian symbol of the trident and wheel, and the infant deity Horus is shown sitting in Indian attitude on a lotus."[49]

Picture: **Pancika** (left) and Hariti (right), holding a cornucopia, 3rd century CE, Takht-i Bahi, British Museum. The legendary Hariti Devi, protector of children and the wife of Panchika were born divinities that were converted to Buddhism by Lord Buddha. Panchika, is also known as Kubera. Kubera is a yaksha, a god of wealth and the hidden treasures of the earth. It is well known that Emperor Ashoka of India, upon becoming a Buddhist convert, was instrumental in the dissemination of the Buddhist teachings throughout the known ancient world. He sent Buddhist missionaries throughout India and to various countries. There are also several iconographical evidences, some mentioned above and others that will be presented later, that link Buddhism with Neterianism, and especially with the temple of Het-ka-Ptah (Memphis) in Egypt.

"Ashoka (c. 291-232 BC), emperor of India He sent missionaries to countries as remote as Greece and Egypt. His reign is known from engravings on rocks and from traditions in Sanskrit literature. He was the most celebrated ruler of ancient India, known for his benevolent rule and for making Buddhism the official religion of his empire. Despite Ashoka's vigorous exertions in behalf of his faith, he was tolerant of other religions, and India enjoyed marked prosperity during his reign."[50]

In the chapter of the book *India and Egypt: Influences and Interactions, 1993*, entitled *Transmission of Ideas and Imagery,* the scholar M. C. Joshi reports on ancient written documents attesting to the communications and cultural exchanges between Ancient Egypt and India during the time of the Indian emperor Ashoka. This record shows not only economic exchanges, but social and humanitarian exchanges, pointing to the compatibility of the two countries. Just as two people who are of opposite character cannot get along, so too countries cannot get along if their peoples are of an opposite nature. Thus, the fact that the Egyptian ruler allowed the contact and allowed Indian artifacts and people into the country without fear of having his power being undermined or that the social order would fail or that the ethnic character would change, etc., as is so often the case in modern government relations which are filled with mistrust, fear and racism, further attests to the compatibility, and likely similarity, of these two cultures.

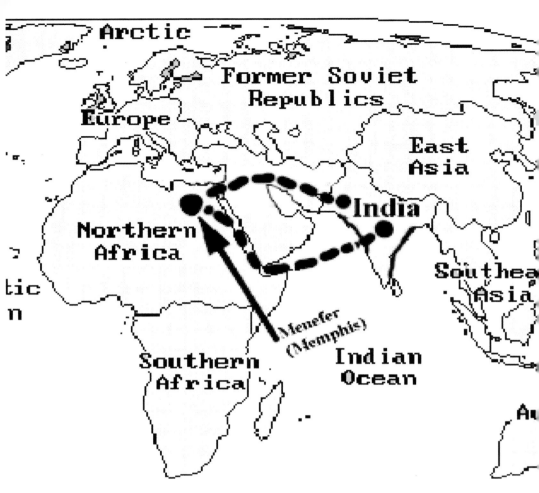

**Above: Trade Routes Between Menefer (Memphis)
Egypt and India**

EARLY INSCRIPTIONS AND LITERARY REFERENCES

The brightest evidence of India's direct relations with Egypt is, however, preserved in the Mauryan Emperor Ashoka's thirteenth rock edict,[51] inscribed in the early decades of the third century BC. In it, Emperor Ashoka refers to his contacts with Ptolemy II Philadelphus of Egypt (285-246 BC), in connection with the expansion of his policy of the propagation of the Law of Righteousness *(dharma)*. In the Ashokan records Ptolemy II is referred to as

Turamaya. There can be little doubt that official embassies were exchanged between the Mauryan court and that of Ptolemy II. Pliny names the Egyptian Ambassador of Ptolemy II to India as Dionysus.[52]

Ashoka, in his second rock edict, refers to the philanthropic activities undertaken by himself. He records that he had made arrangements for the medical treatment of men and animals in the territories of his own empire as well as in the region ruled by Antiochus Theos II of Syria (260-246 BC) and its neighboring kingdoms,[53] which also included Egypt.

Interestingly, it is stated that the Egyptian ruler Ptolemy IV, Philopator, lined a part of his yacht with Indian stones. The presence of Indians in Egypt in the third century BC has been attested by Athenaeus who observes that the processions of Ptolemy II Philadelphus also included women, cows, and hunting dogs from India.[54]

In the chapter of the book *India and Egypt: Influences and Interactions*, 1993, entitled *Transmission of Ideas and Imagery*, the scholar M. C. Joshi reports on ancient written documents attesting to the communications and cultural exchanges between Ancient Egypt and India during the time of the Indian emperor Ashoka.

In the book Search for the Buddha by Charles Allen, the author documents the Buddhist connection to Ancient Egypt as follows. The Buddhist/Indian ruler had a practice of setting up pillars with inscriptions attesting to his following the Buddhist principles and other edicts. One was discovered that unequivocally shows that ancient Egypt and India were associated.

Above: 6thPillarOfAshoka pillar of Ashoka from Brit
Museum

Above: Ashoka's first rock inscription at Girnar { **Girnar**
(also known as "Girnar Hill") is a collection of mountains
in the Junagadh District of Gujarat, India.}

In March 1838 a more complete and accurate impression of the Girnar rock inscription became available to James Prinsep. On 14 'March he wrote another of those letters to Alexander Cunningham that bubble over with enthusiasm and good cheer. The Girnar inscription differed from the pillar edicts in a number of passages, and in one he had found a line that linked Piyadasi/Ashoka to Egypt and the Ptolemys:

The passage in the 14th edict is much mutilated, and I long for a more correct copy. It really becomes interesting to find Egypt and Ptolemy known to Asoka! I must give you the real text:

Yona raja paran cha tena chaptaro rajanan tulamayo
Greek king furthermore by whom the Gypta rajas Ptolemy
*cha antigina cha maga cha * * ***
and Antigonus and Magus and * * *
savata devanampiya dhammanusasti anubatate yata pajati
everywhere Beloved of the God's religious precept reaches where goes.

Hurrah for inscriptions!

Here was proof of diplomatic links between Ashoka's empire and the West, in the form of Alexander the Great's successors: the Egyptian king Ptolemy was probably Ptolemy II (ruled 285-247 BCE); Antigonus was probably Antigonos Gonatos of Macedonia

Above: Main entrance to the ancient Spiritual Center and Temple of Memphis at Sakkara, Egypt, the city where the Buddhist colony was located.

The tantric magical teaching of Menefer [Memphis] was transferred to India through the Tantric Buddhist practices. In China Buddhism and the philosophy of special movements related to animals was instituted by Bodhiharma, a Buddhist practitioner.

The now ruined city of Memphis in Egypt lies beside the Nile River, approximately 19 km/12 mi South of Cairo, Egypt and Sakkara was part of its district in ancient times. Memphis was the center of the worship of the god Ptah, and the heart of Memphite Theology. Memphis was also the earliest capital of a united Egypt under King Menes about 3200 BC, but was superseded by Thebes under the new empire 1570 BC. Memphis was later used as a stone quarry, but the "cemetery city" of Sakkara survives, with the step pyramid built for King Zoser (Djozer) by Imhotep, regarded as the world's oldest stone building.[41] It should be noted here that the Step Pyramid in Sakkara is universally accepted as the oldest of all the Great Pyramids in Egypt. Its superb architecture has also been recognized as the source for the early Greek

Doric forms.[42] This means that based on the now confirmed earlier date for the "Great Pyramid" (see the section "The Revised History of Ancient Egypt Based On New Archeological Evidence and the Omitted Records"), the Old Kingdom Period of Ancient Egypt must be placed in the 5th millennium B.C.E. Also, there was a community of Indians and Buddhists in Memphis in the Late Period of Ancient Egyptian history.[43]   Buddhist records show that early Buddhists had visited Memphis and had set up a settlement there. Henceforth Buddhism begins to develop similar iconographies including the Divinity sitting on the lotus, and also lotus friezes similar to those of Ancient Egypt appear in Buddhist art.

Below: reconstructed section of the main temple at the Djozer complex in Sakkara Egypt {Menefer-Memphis}

Origins of the Hatha Yoga Postures and How they Connect Ancient Egyptian and Tantric Buddhist Spirituality

Short History Of The Yogic Postures in Ancient Egypt and India

The origins of Hatha Yoga have been associated with Tantric Buddhism and not in Hinduism since we find evidence of its early practice by Tantric Buddhists and rejection of Hatha Yoga by the Hindu sages. Hatha Yoga is clearly rejected in the Laghu -Yoga - Vasistha (5.6.86, 92), an early text of Yoga philosophy, which maintains that it merely leads to pain. Some of the criticisms against Hatha Yoga were especially against the magical undercurrents of the practice (Ashby, 2002). Tantric Buddhism gave rise to the earliest practice of certain postures in India as a means to enhance spiritual evolution. Before this time, the only reference to Asana or posture was the sitting posture for meditation, mentioned in the Raja Yoga Sutras by Patanjali. In ancient Kamit there were at least 24 postures in the spiritual practice prior to the time of Patanjali. In the practice of Kamitan *Tjef Neteru* (Egyptian Hatha Yoga, (Ashby, 1999) the "magic"[i] consists in using postures to engender certain alignments with spiritual energies and cosmic forces. This is the kind of practice repudiated by the Hindu sages but adopted by the Tantric Buddhists. Between the years 100 A.C.E. and 1000 A.C.E. the Buddhist Kaula school developed some

---

[i] The term magic is not used in the western sense. Here it means disciplines of transformative power through sound, posture and ritual.

postures. Then Goraksha developed what is regarded by present day Hatha Yoga practitioners as a practice similar to the present day. However, the number of postures only reached 15 at the time of the Hatha Yoga Pradipika scripture. The Mysore family was instrumental in the development since they were strong patrons of Hatha Yoga. Subsequent teachers developed more postures and vinyasa[i] (which was not practiced in early Indian Hatha Yoga) up to the 20th century where there are over 200. The teacher Krishnamacharya said he had learned from a yoga teacher in Tibet. Krishnamacharya's first writings, which cited the Stitattvanidhi as a source, also featured vinyasa [prescribed sequence of postures] that Krishnamacharya said he had learned from a yoga teacher in Tibet. So the practice of the postures in India does not extend to ancient times and did not begin in India with Hinduism but with Buddhism and Buddhism was associated with the Ancient Egyptian city of Memphis where postures and spiritual magic were practiced previously.

---

[i] vinyasa (sequences of poses synchronized with the breath)

Sakkara/Memphis

Above: *Djozer Pyramid Complex* with the *Step Pyramid of Imhotep* located in Sakkara, Egypt– From the Old Kingdom Period – Third Dynasty- School of Memphite Theology- based on the Divinity *Ptah.* The Tantric magical teachings and the Ancient Egyptian postures were absorbed by Tantric Buddhists and that teaching would become Hatha Yoga in Tibet and India and Kung Fu Tai Chi and Chi Kung in China.

TANTRIC
BUDDHIST
"MAGIC"
YOGA
(Tibet – India)

Buddhism
Shaolin-Kung Fu
Tai-Chi
Chi Kung

(China)

Bodhiharma

Buddhist Colony in Sakkara
Egypt

In ancient Kamit (Egypt) the practice of "magic", not the modern entertainment of prestidigitation for entertainment, but the discipline of spiritual practice to transform the personality from lower consciousness to higher, was legendary. Buddhism originally did not have a Tantric tradition but in the early part of the first millennium B.C.E. it developed one. That period was after the direct contact with the teachings of Ancient Egypt.

Since their introduction to the West the exercise system of India known as "Hatha Yoga" has gained much popularity. The disciplines related to the yogic postures and movements were developed in India around the 10th century A.C.E. by a sage named Goraksha.* Up to this time, the main practice was simply to adopt the cross-legged meditation posture known as the lotus for the purpose of practicing meditation. The most popular manual on Hatha Yoga is the *Hatha-Yoga-Pradipika ("Light on the Forceful Yoga)*. It was authored by Svatmarama Yogin in mid. 14th century C.E.**

Below- The god Geb in the plough posture engraved on the ceiling of the antechamber to the Asarian Resurrection room of the Temple of Hetheru in Egypt. (photo taken by Ashby)

Prior to the emergence of the discipline the physical movements in India just before 1000 A.C.E., a series of virtually identical postures to those which were practiced in India can be found in various Ancient Egyptian papyruses and inscribed on the walls and ceilings of the temples. The Ancient Egyptian practice can be dated from 300 B.C.E 1,580 B.C.E and earlier. Exp. Temple of Hetheru (800-300 B.C.E.), Temple of Heru (800-300 B.C.E.), Tomb of Queen Nefertari (reigned 1,279-1,212 BC), Temple of Horemakhet (10,000 B.C.E.) and various other temples and papyruses from the New Kingdom Era 1,580 B.C.E). In Ancient Egypt the practice of the postures (called *Sema Paut* (Union with the gods and goddesses) or *Tjef Sema Paut Neteru* (movements to promote union with the gods and goddesses) were part of the ritual aspect of the spiritual myth which when practiced serve to harmonize the energies and promote the physical health of the body and direct the mind, in a meditative capacity, to discover and cultivate divine consciousness. These disciplines are part of a larger process called Sema or *Smai Tawi* (Egyptian Yoga). By acting and moving like the gods and goddesses one can essentially discover their character, energy and divine agency within one's consciousness and thereby also become one of their retinue, i.e. one with the Divine Self. In modern times, most practitioners of Hatha Yoga see it

90

means to attain physical health only. However, even the practice in India had a mythic component which is today largely ignored.

(Below) In the upper right hand corner of the ceiling of the Peristyle Hall in the Temple of Aset a special image of the goddess Nut and the God Geb and the higher planes of existence can be seen. Nut and Geb. Below: -line drawing of the same scene. (Temple of Aset {Isis}).

The figure at left depicts another conceptualization of the Netherworld, which is at the same time the body of Nut in a forward bend posture.

The god Geb is on the ground practicing the Plough Yoga exercise posture. The goddess in the center symbolizes the lower heaven in which the moon traverses, the astral realm. The outermost goddess symbolizes the course of the sun in its astral journey and the causal plane.

Notice the characteristic Nubian headdress of Nut, which is also visible in the iconography of Bas. This iconography links the late Kamitan religion with that of the Pre-Dynastic era, and with the Nubian origins of Kamitan culture. Geb, who is in the plough posture, symbolizes the physical plane and all solid matter, while the goddesses represent the subtler levels of existence.

Records of <u>meditation as a discipline for lay people, as opposed to priests,</u> first show up about 500 B.C. in both

India and China. Contrary to what many Yoga students believe, his (Patanjali) text said little about Hatha Yoga postures, which weren't a widespread practice at the time. It only speaks of a sitting posture for the practice of meditation and nothing more.

From Raja Yoga Sutras – Translated by Swami Jyotirmayananda:
    Samadhi Pad Sutra 46: *seated pose for meditation*
Samadhi Pad Sutra 48-49: *perfecting the seated pose for meditation*

Below: The Egyptian Gods and Goddesses assume special postures that manifest their particular cosmic power. (taken from Ancient Egyptian reliefs, papyri, temple inscriptions and other Ancient Egyptian sources.

THE SMAI TAWI (EGYPTIAN YOGA) POSTURES

1-Uah Khepri Time before Creation
2- Creation-Nefertem
3- Creation-Nun
4-Warm Up
5- Shu Air-Space
6- Udja Ra Journey of Ra
7- Geb-Plough Earth
8- The Wheel
9- The Fish of Ra
10-Forward Bend
11- Geb Spinal Twist
12-Selket the scorpion
13-Sobek the crocodile
14-Asar the cobra
15-Horemakhet the sphinx
16-Heru Master of Nature
17- Henu adorations
18- Nut expansion, infinity
19- Maat Order, balance
20-Aset wisdom, intuition
21-Aset Divine Throne
22- Divine Embrace
23-Djed Divine Pillar
24- Hea
26-Asar, Mummy

Above: The varied postures found in the Kemetic papyruses and temple inscriptions. (Egyptian Yoga Postures Poster)

Below- the Goddess Parvati from India, practicing the tree Pose – modern rendition (20th Cent.).

While the practice of the Tjef Neteru [Ancient Egyptian pyoga postures] was associated with the gods and goddesses from ancient times [before 2,000 B.C.E.0 Only at about the year 1,700 A.C.E. did the Shiva Samhita text Associate Hatha Yoga With the god and goddess Shiva and Parvati (Shakti)

Many people do not know that when the practice of Hatha Yoga was adopted by yogis (one who studies the yoga disciplines) in India in the first millennium A.C.E., it was repudiated by the established practitioners. When it was opened up to the general community and ceased to be a practice of secluded yogis and was later brought to the west at the turn of the 20th century much later, it was not quickly adopted. However, in the latter part of the 20th century, due to the ardent promotion by a few Indian masters, it has gained wide notoriety. However, for the most part only the physical benefits have been adopted and acknowledged while the mystical teachings within the discipline have not been embraced generally. Beyond the misinformed and the dogmatic followers of orthodox religion, who repudiate yoga as an occult, evil practice, one comment by a famous personality in late 20th century western culture typifies the feeling of the vast majority of those who are involved in yoga for the physical "benefits" other than "spiritual" aspects of yoga:

"I don't want it to change my life, just my butt."
-famous actress (United States-2000 A.C.E.)**

Still, it must be understood that many people who are leading a worldly life are first introduced to yoga through the discipline of the postures in ordinary sessions dedicated to promoting physical health and later turn towards the spiritual aspects. However, there is much concern among advanced practitioners of Yoga in India and elsewhere, that Western culture has appropriated yoga and converted it to something other than yoga as it has been known for thousands of years. Instead of having Geb or Parvati as the role models, such prominent (worldly) personalities as actors and entertainers Julia Roberts, Madonna, Woody Haroldson and others have become the "ideal." So now, the same materialistic pursuits (physical health, beauty, sex-appeal, excitement, etc.), which are the hallmarks of western culture, have been projected on yoga by westerners who have appointed themselves as the purveyors of yoga to the masses. Many also distribute a myriad of products which are not necessary or desirable for the practice of yoga postures such as spandex, props, lotions, bikini yoga, etc., and conduct not spiritual yoga retreats but yoga vacations, yoga parties and the like. Yoga originated as a non-secular spiritual discipline for transcending the world and has now been converted by many into a means to enjoy the worldly pleasures more intensely. This deviation from spiritual discipline to an instrument for enhancing worldly pleasure-seeking is perhaps most prominently visible in the discipline of Tantra Yoga. Using sexual symbolism to drive home a mystical teaching, Tantra Yoga has less to do with physical sexual intercourse between human beings than intercourse of the soul with the Divine. Yet, many so called practitioners of Tantra Yoga in the west tirelessly promote the idea that it is a form of "Sex-Yoga" designed to attain spiritual enlightenment and the heights of worldly pleasure at the same time. There are many misconceptions about the history and teaching of yoga and this is perhaps one of the most blatant. The hedonistic* path of life, which typifies western culture, has been shown to be ultimately a dead end street leading to frustration and regret in later life. Yet people follow blindly the inane statements of ignorant religious leaders, entertainers, politicians, marketers and advertisers, which lead to spiritual and worldly bankruptcy.

In the present, practitioners of the Hatha Yoga postures do not realize that the postures were not designed just to promote physical health. Actually, like the Kemetic system, the Hindu Yoga posture system is also designed to relate a human being to the gods and goddesses and the cosmic forces, which are symbolized by the use of animal names and visualizations using natural objects. This is accomplished by the practice of the movements, study of the mythology and philosophy behind them and meditative absorption with the principles and energies that they represent. The promotion of health is only a means to an end, a byproduct of the practice, and not an end in itself.

The ultimate goal of yoga is to awaken the spiritual consciousness. Any other use of yoga is a misuse or at least a limited use. In these respects the movement systems of Kemet {Kamit} from Ancient Egypt, Yoga from India, and Kung Fu of China, are unique when compared to other forms of exercise, movement systems. Western forms of exercise are designed to cultivate the external muscles and physical energy while the Eastern and African disciplines are designed to develop and cultivate the internal life force, which transcends physicality and the world itself.

SECTION NOTES:

Yoga Journal, {The New Yoga} January/February 2000

Hatha-Yoga-Pradipika, *The Shambhala Encyclopedia of Yoga* by Georg
    Feuerstein, Ph. D.

The Shambhala Encyclopedia of Yoga by Georg Feuerstein, Ph. D.

The Shambhala Encyclopedia of Yoga by Georg Feuerstein, Ph. D.

Yoga Journal, {The New Yoga} January/February 2000

The Postures below are the basic positions that are used in Indian Hatha Yoga. The strong similarities to the Ancient Egyptian postures will be noticed.

Time-line of Ancient Egypt, Early Buddhism and Hatha Yoga Postures

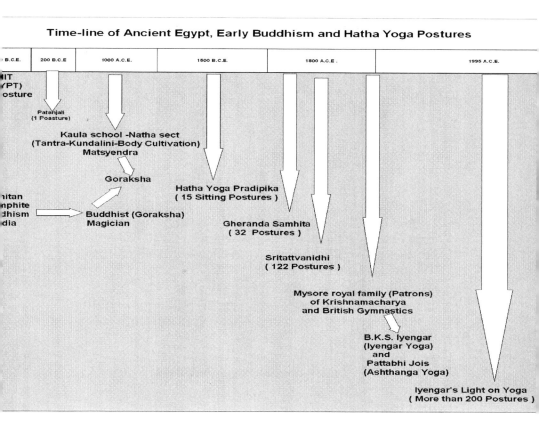

This timeline indicates the early process of evolution of Hatha Yoga in India. Hatha Yoga is said to have been originated from the Buddhist Tantric practitioners. The discipline of spiritual postures was already practiced, along with, spiritual magic, in Ancient Egypt when the Buddhist practitioners arrived in Egypt. It shows the dates in which the practice of spiritual postures was enjoined in Africa and Asia. The earliest recorded evidence for the practice of specific movements that lead to spiritual enlightenment occurs in Ancient Egypt (Kamit) c. 10,000 B.C.E. The earliest recorded practice in India of the yoga postures is c. 1,000 A.C.E.

The following list summarizes the dates in which the practice of spiritual postures was enjoined in Africa and Asia. The earliest recorded evidence for the practice of specific movements that lead to spiritual enlightenment occurs in Ancient Egypt (Kamit) c. 10,000 B.C.E. The earliest recorded practice in India of the yoga postures is c. 1,000 A.C.E.

Timeline Summary (1800 B.C.E.-1000 A.C.E.)

1,800 B.C.E. Ancient Egypt – Discipline of Sema Paut-Egyptian Yoga Postures, Arat Shetaut Neter (Goddess Mysteries), Arat Sekhem (Serpent Power), Hekau ("Magic) Already ancient.

550 B.C.E. Cambyses invades Egypt – Buddhism, Jainism, Pythagoreaninsm, Zoroastrianism, Confucianism, Taoism - BORN

261 B.C.E. Buddhist associations with Ancient Egypt – colony in Memphis.

100 A.C.E. -Tantrism – Emerges as a Distinct culture of Spirituality in Hinduism, Buddhism and Jainism Emphasizing Shaktism (Goddess female energy and Goddess as female aspect of the Absolute), Occultism, Magic, Kundalini

c. 460-490 A.C.E. Shakta and Tantra Spirituality -Writings elaborating on Tantric spirituality and mysticism of the Chakras

1000 A.C.E. -Goraksha – Develops Hatha Yoga to "Force" the movement of Kundalini (serpent Power) # of Postures?

1995 A.C.E. Iyengar developed more than 200 postures.

Buddhist and Egyptian Iconography of Buddha

Above top: Sculpture of an Ancient Egyptian Official from Sakkara (Old Kingdom) Brooklyn Museum

Above Below: Kamitan-Kushitic sculpture, described by the Brooklyn Museum as "Black man." (Hellenistic period)

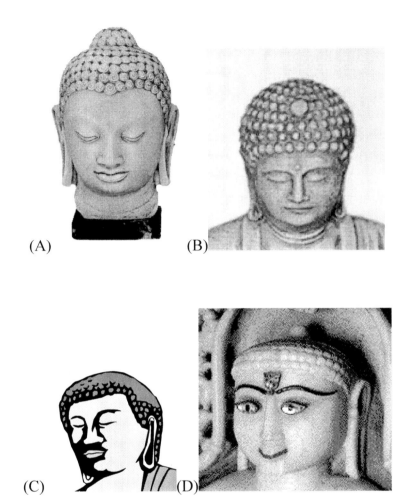

Above (A) Early Buddha sculpture now at the Sarnath Museum India 450 A.C.E., (B) and (C) Buddha of India, (D) Mahavira – from the Jain Temple at Jaiselmer, India.

Introduction to Fundamental Buddhist Philosophy

An overview of Buddhist philosophy will provide insights into its relationship with Buddhism and Kamitan (Ancient Egypt) religious philosophy.

<u>The Setting in Motion of the Wheel of the Law:</u>

<u>The Noble Truth of Suffering is:</u>

The reason for all suffering is participation in the world process:

One is unhappy because one invariably expects to find happiness in worldly things.

<u>The Noble Truth of the Cause of Suffering:</u>

The cause of suffering is <u>Ignorance</u> (Avidya).
You have a fundamental misconception about reality.
I see no other single hindrance such as this hindrance of IGNORANCE, obstructed by which mankind for a long, long time runs on, round and round in circles (Ittivutaka).

<u>The Noble Truth of the End of Suffering:</u>

The End of Suffering is ENLIGHTENMENT (NIRVANA).
The way to Nirvana is the basis of Buddha's teaching.

<u>The Noble Eight-fold Path:</u>

The Noble Eight-fold Path is the practical means to disentangle the knot of ignorance and illusion.

<u>1- Right Understanding</u> is learning how to see the world as it truly is.

2- Right Thought is understanding that thought has great power on oneself and others and that whatever one focuses on gains more life; one becomes it.
3- Right Speech is knowing what to say, how to say it, when to say it, and when to remain silent.
4- Right Action: Guidelines for controlling one's behavior and allowing calmness of mind to pursue Enlightenment:

> *1. Not intentionally taking the life of any creature.*
> *2. Not taking anything which is not freely given.*
> *3. Not indulging in irresponsible sexual behavior.*
> *4. Not speaking falsely, abusively or maliciously.*
> *5. Not consuming alcohol or drugs.*

5- Right Livelihood is making a living in such a way as to benefit oneself and all other beings.
6- Right Effort is determination and perseverance in one's spiritual discipline to transcend one's lower nature.
7- Right Mindfulness is learning how to be aware of everything that one does at all times, not acting automatically, reacting to events as an animal.

8- Right Meditation is a way to transcend into higher forms of consciousness including:

> *"The four stages with form" and*
> *"The four stages without form."*

These comprise successive levels of introvertedness:

> *Joy, Equanimity, and Mindfulness.*

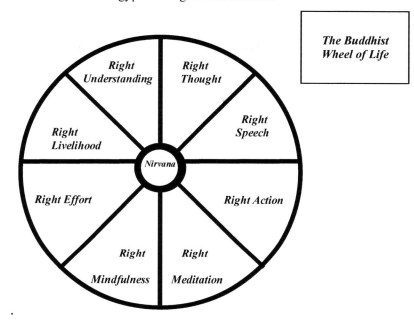

The Symbols and Teachings of Enlightenment in India and Ancient Egypt

In light of the mounting evidence linking Buddhism with Ancient Egyptian Religion, it should be noted that the term "Buddha," meaning "enlightened one" relates to the concept that spiritual ignorance is like a form of darkness and that spiritual knowledge is like a light which illumines the mind and shines on one's innermost soul. The Buddhist term "Bodha" or "enlightenment" is synonymous with the terms "Awakening," "Self-Realization" and "Liberation." Though the use of the term "Enlightenment" was popularized by the discipline of Buddhism as a means to highlight this concept, it was also used in Ancient Egypt in the remote periods of antiquity. In Buddhism, the Transcendental consciousness is likened to a light and Buddha Consciousness is understood as wakefulness or awareness of that light. Thus, anyone who achieves that form of illumination is called a "Buddha."

The Concept of Sitting on the Lotus

The Lotus Symbol of Ancient Egypt and Indian Hinduism

Above: Left-Lotus from Egypt

Above: Right: Indian Lotus

Below- The God Heru (left) and the god Krishna/Brahma (right) sitting on the lotus.

The symbolic usage of the lotus we just saw in the previous item for comparison is taken to another level when the correlations between the lotuses of Egypt and India are examined more closely. First, in both mythologies the lotus symbolizes the number 1,000 (manifold). Since the lotus opens and turns towards the light of the sun, it is a natural symbol in both Neterianism and Hinduism of turning towards the light of the Divine Spirit. Further, the lotus symbolizes dispassion in both mythologies as it grows in the muddy waters but remains untouched by the waters due to a special coating. So too a spiritual aspirant must remain detached from the world even while continuing to live and work in it, while at the same time turning away from the world and towards the Divine. In both mythologies the symbol is used to represent the creation itself, which emerges out of the murky, disordered waters of primeval potential in order to establish order and truth and make a way for life. The lotus also symbolizes the glorious fragrance of the Divine Self as well as the state of spiritual enlightenment. Thus, the symbol that was first used in Ancient Egypt was adopted in India, and though the name changes from Seshen (Kamitan - a source for the English name "Susan") to Padma (Hindu) its symbolism, number, myth and usage remained the same.

Below left- Amunhotep, son of Hapu, Ancient Egyptian philosopher, priest and Sage at 80 years old in a meditative posture. Below right - Buddha "The Enlightened One" of India.

Ancient Egyptian Wisdom teaching:

"Passions and irrational desires are ills exceedingly great; and over these GOD hath set up the Mind to play the part of judge and executioner."

Buddhist teaching: Nirvana means

"Enlightened Consciousness, Bliss when the mind is free of all desire

Below: Hieroglyphic text for the Ancient Egyptian Book of Enlightenment

"Rau   nu   Prt   M   Hr   u"

What is The Rau nu Pert em Hru?

The scriptures commonly known as the *Egyptian Book of the Dead* contain the philosophy and technology or the *"technical yoga practices"* for attaining enlightenment. These texts span the entire history of Ancient Egypt, beginning with the *Pyramid Texts* in the early Dynastic Period. These were followed by the *Coffin Texts*, which were followed by the middle and late Dynastic texts which were recorded on a variety of different media, of which the most popularly known is papyrus.

The teachings of mystical spirituality are contained in the most ancient writings of Ancient Egypt, even those preceding the Dynastic or Pharaonic period (4,500 B.C.E.-600 A.C.E). The most extensive expositions of the philosophy may be found in the writings, which have in modern times been referred to as "The Egyptian Book of the Dead." It was originally known as "Rau nu Prt M Hru" or "Rau nu *Pert Em Heru*" or "Reu nu *Pert Em Heru*."

> *Rau=* words, teachings, liturgy, *nu* = of, *Prt* or *Pert* = going out, *em* or *m* = as or through, *Hru* or *Heru* = Spiritual Light or Enlightened Being (the God Heru). This may therefore be translated as: *"The Word Utterances for Coming into the Spiritual Light (Enlightenment) or Becoming one with Heru (the light)."*

Thus, the *Rau nu Pert Em Heru* is a collection of words used to affirm spiritual wisdom and to direct a human being towards a positive spiritual movement. Each *Rau* or *Ru* contains affirmations of mystical wisdom and or practices that enable a human being to understand and experience that particular aspect of Divinity. The collection of these verses has been referred to as "Chapters," "Utterances" or "Spells" by Egyptologists. While the teachings presented in the *Rau nu Pert Em Heru* may be thought of as being presented in Chapters and referred to as such, they must also be thought of as special words which, when understood, internalized and lived, will lead a person to spiritual freedom. In this sense they are equal to the Hindu concept of "Sutras," short verses or formulas of spiritual wisdom or as "mantras," words of power. "Chapters" may be better defined as: a collection of Hekau -words of power- which impart a spiritual teaching and affirm that teaching, and by their repeated utterance make it a reality. The term "Ru" may be used as a shortened version of "Rau." It was not until after 1,500 B.C.E. that the collections of Ru were compiled in the form of papyrus scrolls and standardized to some degree. However, this process of standardization was not as rigid as the canonization of the books of the Bible, which had been separate scriptures relating to Christianity and Judaism prior to around the year 350 A.C.E.

In Egyptian myth, Hru is not only a reference to the god who is the son of Aset and Asar (Isis and Osiris), but Hru also means "Day" and "Light." In fact, Day and Light are two of the most important attributes of the god Heru who is understood as the highest potential of every human being. Therefore, the title may also be read as **"The Book of Coming Forth by (into) the Day," "The Guide for Becoming Heru,"** i.e. One with God, **"The Chapters for Coming into the Light,"** or **"The Book of Enlightenment."** The writings were named "The Egyptian Book of the Dead" by modern Egyptologists who obtained them from the modern day dwellers of the area (northeast African Arabs) who said they were found buried with the Ancient Egyptian dead.

Many people think of the philosophy of Enlightenment as a concept that originated in India, with the teachings of *Moksha* (Liberation), especially with Buddhism. We have shown that it is a concept that was well understood in ancient Kamit and is very much in harmony with what is today referred to as Enlightenment. In Ancient Egypt the terms for enlightenment were Nehast (resurrect-wake up) or Pert m Heru "coming into the light (i.e. enlightenment)"

Resurrection, spiritual Enlightenment- *Nehast*

The Kamitan term "nehast" (resurrection) is derived from the Kamitan word "Nehas" meaning "to wake up, Awaken."

Awaken - *Nehas*

Definition of Enlightenment (common to Neterianism, Hinduism {Vedanta}, Buddhism and Taoism):

Enlightenment is the term used to describe the highest level of spiritual awakening. It means attaining such a level of spiritual awareness that one discovers the underlying unity of the entire universe as well as the fact that the source of all creation is the same source from which the innermost Self within every human heart arises. It is a state of ecstasy and bliss which transcends all concepts and descriptions and which does not diminish and is not affected by the passage of time or physical conditions. It is in the state of Enlightenment that the absolute proof of the teachings of mystical spirituality are to be found and not in books, doctrines or dogmas. This is because intellectual knowledge is only the beginning of the road which leads to true knowledge. There are two forms of knowledge, intellectual (theoretical) and absolute (experiential). The teachings of Yoga and the advanced stages of religion can lead a person to experience the truth about the transcendental, immortal and eternal nature of the Soul and the existence of God. This is what differentiates Yoga from intellectual philosophies and debates, cults or religious dogma. In Yoga there is no exhortation to believe in anything other than what you can prove through your own experience. In order to do this, all that is necessary is to follow the disciplines which have been scientifically outlined since many thousands of years ago. The state of enlightenment may be summarized as follows:

> "Enlightenment means attaining that sublime and highest goal of life which is complete Self-knowledge, to experience the state of conscious awareness of oneness with the Divine and all Creation which transcends individuality born of ego consciousness...like the river uniting with the ocean, discovering the greater essential nature of Self... that state which bestows abiding blessedness, peace, bliss, contentment, fulfillment, freedom from all limitation and supreme empowerment."

Buddhist Dharma Philosophy and Ancient Egyptian Maat Philosophy

The philosophy of the Eight-fold path has striking similarities to the concepts of Maat. This agreement is likely a product of the close relationship between India and Egypt during the time of Herodotus, and especially in the time of the Indian Emperor Ashoka. The Eight-fold path is based on the philosophy that life is suffering. The reason for all suffering is participation in the world process. One is unhappy because one invariably expects to find happiness in worldly objects and situations. Thus, one develops feelings of desire for things and fear of losing them. All life is sorrowful. Even pleasurable moments are sorrowful because they set us up for disappointment later on at some point since conditions of life always change and all attainments are ultimately ephemeral.

The following table contains a comparison of some of the most important Buddhist and Ancient Egyptian Religious philosophies. They are compared to demonstrate their compatibility.

Fundamental Buddhist Philosophy 600 B.C.E.-100 A.C.E.	Neterian Religion 5,500 B.C.E-450 A.C.E
Avidya. The Noble Truth about the Cause of Suffering is Ignorance. A person has a fundamental misconception about reality. There is no other single hindrance such as this impediment of ignorance.	**On Ignorance** *qmn* "O people of the earth, men and women born and made of the elements, but with the spirit of the Divine within you, rise from your sleep of ignorance! Be sober and thoughtful. Realize that your home is not on the earth but in the Light. Why have you delivered yourselves unto death, having power to partake of immortality? Repent, and change your minds. Depart from the dark light and forsake corruption forever. Prepare to blend your souls with the Eternal Light." (see also the proverb below)
Ittivutaka Because of ignorance a human being experiences a cycle of suffering through reincarnation for a long, long time running around and around in circles. The Noble Truth of the End of Suffering is NIRVANA ("Mind without Desires" - Contentment — Enlightenment).	**On Reincarnation** *Uhem ankh* According to the Pert M Hru text, Uhem Ankh occurs when a person has not attained Nehast or "awakening: sufficient to Pert m Hru "go into the light" due to ignorance.

Nirvana, or Nibbana

Nirvana, or Nibbana, is the Buddhist term signifying the indescribable state attained by enlightened Sages and Saints. In Buddhism, Nirvana is the extinction of craving; in Hinduism, it is the home of liberated souls united with the divine and in Jainism, it is the place of liberated souls. Upon death, Enlightenment is completed in the state of Parinirvana. From a psychological perspective, Nirvana is the psychological position where one has transcended and is indifferent to elation, desire for things or the fear of their loss. The way to Nirvana is the basis of Buddha's teaching.

Bodha

The Buddhist term "Bodha" or one who has "enlightened" intellect is synonymous with the

 *Nehast*

Resurrection, spiritual Enlightenment is a state attained by those who have awakened fully to the truth, that they are more than mortal, limited beings. It is the supreme victory over Set (egoism) that frees the soul to discover its oneness with the transcendental self, *Ptah-Sokkar-Asar.*

The Being of Light *Akhu*

The hieroglyph of the word Akhu or Khu is the "crested ibis." The ibis is representative symbol of Djehuti, the god of reason and knowledge. As such it relates to the pure spiritual essence of a human being that is purified by lucidity of mind. The

terms "Awakening," "Self-Realization" and "Liberation."	Khu is the spirit, which is immortal. The Khu is also referred to as the "being of light" or "luminous being." A person who has discovered the light of spirit being, i.e. *Neberdjer* (all-encompassing transcendental consciousness) is referred to as Akhu.
Anatman Buddhism analyzes human existence as made up of five aggregates or "bundles" (*skandhas*): the material body, feelings, perceptions, predispositions or karmic tendencies, and consciousness. A person is only a temporary combination of these aggregates, which are subject to continual change.	**Ancient Egyptian Proverb on the nature of human existence:** "An infant's Soul is altogether a thing of beauty to see, not yet befouled by body's passions, still all but hanging from the Cosmic Soul! But when the body grows in bulk and draweth down the Soul into it's mass, then doth the Soul cut off itself and bring upon itself forgetfulness, and no more shareth in the Beautiful and Good (God); and this forgetfulness (ignorance) becometh vice."
Karma Term used in the Vedas to mean ritual act. Term used in the Upanishads and later in Buddhism to mean mysticism of actions leading to rebirth for ignorant souls.[58]	**The Concept of Ari** In Ancient Egyptian spirituality the concept of Ari held that the mysticism behind actions is their effect of causing the fate after death and possible rebirth if the soul remains ignorant.

Samsara	Ancient Egyptian Proverb on the world of human existence and rebirth:
Earlier Upanishadic meaning- the world of experience and later Buddhist meaning- rebirth leads to sorrow due to ignorance.	"Salvation is the freeing of the soul from its bodily fetters; becoming a God through knowledge and wisdom; controlling the forces of the cosmos instead of being a slave to them; subduing the lower nature and through awakening the higher self, ending the cycle of rebirth and dwelling with the Neters who direct and control the Great Plan."

On the Following page-Table: Maat Philosophy Compared with Buddhist Dharma Philosophy

Maat Principles of Ethical Conduct	Buddhist Dharma and the Noble Eig Fold Path
The Kamitan Path of Maat 42 Precepts and the Wisdom Texts[59]	**The Noble Eight-fold Path:** The Noble Eight-fold Path is the practical means to disentangle the knot of ignorance and illusion in order to attain Spiritual Enlightenment.
• **Truth: Maat is Right Action-** Understanding the nature of the Divine, right from wrong as well as reality from unreality. • **Non-violence:** This is the philosophy of Imhotep, Akhnaton, Ptahotep and other Kamitan Sages, (approaching life in peace) and Ari-m-hetep (performing actions in peace and contentment. • **Right Action- self-control:** Living in accordance with the teachings of Maat. (integrity, honesty) • **Right Speech** speaking truth and refraining from angry speech. • **Right Worship:** Correct practice of religion including devotional practice, chanting, meditation, donating to the temple. • **Selfless Service:** Service to humanity includes taking care of the homeless, clotheless, the hungry and needy. • **Balance of Mind - Reason – Right Thinking:** Keeping the mind in balance so as not to lose the faculty of rational cognition. This involves a close	• **Right Understanding** is learning how to see the world as it truly is. • **Right Thought** is understanding that thought has great power on oneself and others, and that whatever one focuses on gains more life; one becomes it. • **Right Speech** is knowing what to say, how to say it, when to say it, and when to remain silent. • **Right Action:** Guidelines for controlling one's behavior and allowing calmness of mind to pursue Enlightenment: Not intentionally taking the life of any creature. (non-violence) Not taking anything which is not freely given. Not indulging in irresponsible sexual behavior. Not speaking falsely, abusively or maliciously. Not consuming alcohol or drugs.

attention (mindfulness) to control, prevent and eradicate the egoistic tendencies of the mind (arrogance, conceit, self-importance, greed, etc.).

- **Not-stealing:** Stealing is a socially disruptive practice which denotes the degraded level of human consciousness and reinforces the ignorance of worldly desire and pleasure-seeking as well as greed.
- **Sex-Sublimation:** Sexuality is one of the primal forces of nature which must be controlled in order to allow the personality to discover the higher perspectives of life.
- **Maat Offering:** By acting with righteousness and attaining virtue the supreme offering is made through the Maat Offering in which the person making the offering enters into a meditative awareness through the ritual and sees {him/her} self as becoming one with Maat.

- **Right Livelihood** is making a living in such a way as to benefit oneself and all other beings.
- **Right Effort** is determination and perseverance in one's spiritual discipline to transcend one's lower nature.
- **Right Mindfulness** is learning how to be aware of everything that one does at all times, not acting automatically, reacting to events as an animal.
- **Right Meditation** is a way to transcend into higher forms of consciousness including: "The four stages with form" and "The four stages without form." These comprise successive levels of introvertedness: Joy, Equanimity, and Mindfulness.

At the level where Buddha Consciousness is reached, it is now possible to live and participate in the world though remaining completely detached from it. This concept is that of the Bodhisattva who, out of compassion, helps others on their spiritual journey to achieving Buddha Consciousness. This philosophy is known as: *"Joyful participation in the sorrows of the world."*[60] This philosophy is not unlike Jesus' compassion for the world by willingly submitting to the pain of life in order to show the path to the Kingdom of Heaven through selfless service and humanitarianism. Also, this philosophy is not unlike Asar's (God of Ancient Egypt-

See below) compassion for the world as he incarnated at the request of Ra in order to show humanity how to become civilized. He too suffered for the sake of humanity. The Yoga system of Maat from Kamit, and of Patanjali and the Philosophy of Buddha of India, represent the many paths to union with the Divine, which may be used according to the psychological makeup (character) of the individual. This philosophy of service to humanity, as opposed to leaving humanity and dwelling in isolation, is one of the hallmarks of Kamitan culture. Priests and Priestesses were required to

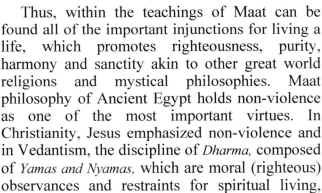

serve the laity in various capacities, ministerial, medical, legal, etc., and at the same time their duties to the Temple were maintained in a balanced manner.

Thus, within the teachings of Maat can be found all of the important injunctions for living a life, which promotes righteousness, purity, harmony and sanctity akin to other great world religions and mystical philosophies. Maat philosophy of Ancient Egypt holds non-violence as one of the most important virtues. In Christianity, Jesus emphasized non-violence and in Vedantism, the discipline of *Dharma,* composed of *Yamas and Nyamas,* which are moral (righteous) observances and restraints for spiritual living, emphasizes non-violence also. The Ancient Egyptian, Vedantic and Buddhist mystical traditions were the first to recognize the power of non-violence to heal the anger and hatred within the aggressor as well as the victim. When this spiritual force is developed, it is more formidable than any kind of physical violence. Therefore, anyone who wishes to promote peace and harmony in the world must begin by purifying every bit of negativity within themselves. This is the only way to promote true harmony and peace in others. Conversely, if there is anger within one, anger is still being promoted outside of oneself and one's efforts to encourage peace will be unsuccessful in the end.

The Lotus Symbol of Ancient Egypt and India

Below: Blue Lotus panel. Stupa (Buddhist) at Bharhut. 2nd Cent. BC Indian Museum Calcutta

Below: Samples of Ancient Egyptian Blue Lotus Panels. The finding of the blue lotus in Egypt and India in a spiritual context is remarkable since it does not appear in localities in between.

Notice that in between the Blue Lotuses[i] of the Buddhist panel there are "step" pyramids. This is exactly the type of pyramid that was created and venerated in the city of Memphis in Ancient Egypt (5000-3000 B.C.E.).

Above: Tourists visiting the Step Pyramid from Sakkara/Memphis, Egypt (late 20th century)

---

[i] The **Blue Waterlily** (*Nymphaea caerulea*), also known as the Egyptian Blue Lotus or Blue Lotus, is a blue water-lily in the genus *Nymphaea* that grows upon the Nile, amongst other locations. –Wikipedia Encyclopedia

Below -Indian-Buddhist -*Vandevatas* -wood spirits- giving drink from the tree. Bharhut, Sunga 2nd Cent. B.C.E.

{See next page}

Below- left, Nefertum/Asar emerges, resurrected, from the Divine Lotus - Ancient Egypt. Papyrus Ani. Below right- Aspirant receives sustenance from the tree. Ancient Egyptian Papyrus Nu

There are two important motifs in common here between Ancient Egyptian and Buddhist lconographies. The first is the concept of the life-giving tree, which dispenses food and drink. The other is the blue Lotus motif. From Ancient times the symbol of the tree goddess (see next two pages- Goddess Nut gives sustenance to initiate Ani {Any Papyrus- 18th Dynasty-Ancient Egypt) as the life-giving and life sustaining divinity was used in Ancient Egypt as a metaphor of purity in food, from vegetables, but also receiving the food of divine life, wisdom from the goddess, directly from her teachings, which are the fruits of her tree.

Below Left: (A) The god Nefertum of Egypt, sitting on a Lotus. (B) Buddha of India, sitting on a Lotus. (C) Naga Buddha of Angkor Wat (Temple) in Cambodia, sitting on a serpent.

(A) (B)

(C)

The images above reveal another correlation between Memphite iconography and Buddhist iconography. Nefertum (A) is the son of Ptah, the high god at Memphis. Nefertum sits on the lotus from which he speaks the world into existence (Creation). The Creation is the lotus itself upon which Nefertum sits.

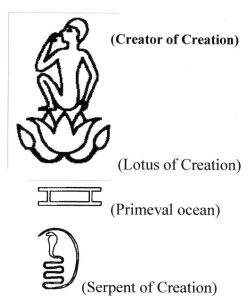

(Creator of Creation)

(Lotus of Creation)

(Primeval ocean)

(Serpent of Creation)

In Ancient Egyptian religion, the lotus of Creation emerges out of the primeval ocean which is stirred by the Mehen Serpent, a gigantic beast whose movements churn the ocean into transforming itself into the various forms of Creation as water turns to ice when it reaches a low enough temperature. In Buddhist myth the same conceptualization is given to Buddha as it is derived, like many other concepts, from Hindu theism, specifically that of Brahma, the Creator who sits on a lotus, which also comes out of the primeval ocean, in order to bring Creation into being. So the concept of the Serpent, the churning of the primeval ocean out of which a lotus emerges with a being who sits atop of it are all common to the Neterian, Hindu and Buddhist traditions.

Below: The Ancient Egyptian God Khepri displays the same concept of "resting" on the serpent power.

Above Left: Heru (Nefertem) on the Lotus, Above Right: Buddha on the Lotus

Buddhism and Neterianism – the divinity Buddha and the god Asar.

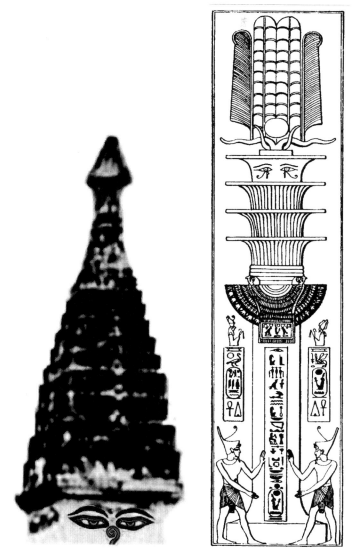

Above left- a Buddhist temple[61]

The Buddhist Temple displays the levels of heaven or states of spiritual consciousness, above the head of Buddha.

Note the eyes of Buddha. The tiers represent levels of spiritual consciousness and these lead one to experience varied levels of experience beyond the physical realm.

Above right- a Kamitan artifact known as the Djed Pillar

The Djed Pillar is one of the primary symbol/artifacts of the god Asar. It displays the levels of heaven or states of spiritual consciousness, as the backbone and head of Asar. Note the eyes of Asar-Heru. In the myth when he was killed, Asar's coffin turned into a tree (tree of life). Then the tree was cut into a pillar through which Asar looked out on the world. The pillar was discovered by the goddess Aset, she cut it open and found his body in it which she resurrected. The Djed was thereafter a symbol of resurrection and glory, the raising of the four upper psycho-spiritual consciousness centers.

The Ankh Symbol in Ancient Egypt and India (Hinduism and Buddhism)

The Ankh, 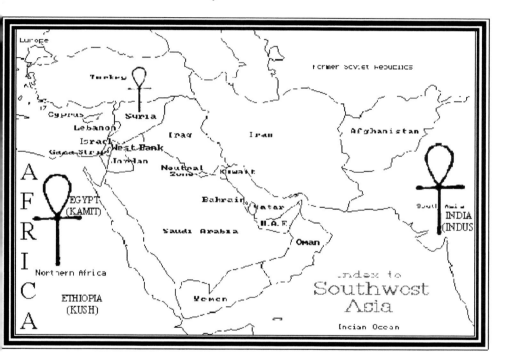, is one of the most recognizable Kamitan symbols. It signifies the life process which sustains creation and living beings. It can be seen in the earliest Kamitan reliefs, and it was adopted by the early Christians who then converted it into the present day Christian Cross. Many people do not know that it was also used by the early Indians with the same symbolism.

Above- a map of North-east Africa and South-east Asia.

This map shows the most important geographical areas where the Ankh symbol was used. It was first used in Africa by the Ancient Egyptians. In India it was used by the Indian mystics and in the Asia minor it was used by the early Christians who practiced Christian Gnosticism (Mystical Christianity).[62]

Below – The Feet of Buddha, displaying the Kamitan Ankh Symbol

In the book *Migration of Symbols,* Count Goblet D' Alviella, discovered the correlation of the cross symbol on the image of the "feet of Buddha" with the "Ankh" symbol of Ancient Egypt, that is more commonly known as the "Key of Life" or "Ankh Cross" or "crux ansata."

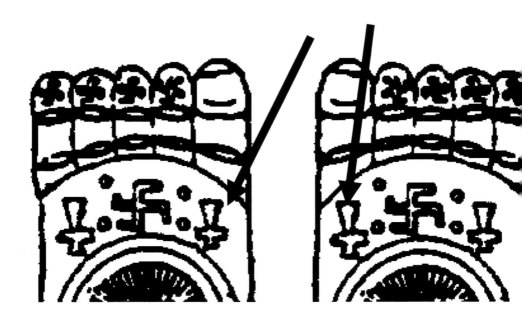

The combination of the *crux ansata* with the Sacred Cone seems to have penetrated as far as India, if this conclusion may be drawn from an enigmatical figure to be seen amongst the symbols carved, at Amaravati, on the feet of Buddha (fig. a. below).

a   *b*

To be sure, the Disk, or oval handle, which surmounts the Cone, is replaced, in the Buddhist symbol, by a triangular handle, or the section of a second cone inverted. But this difference is another presumption in favour of our thesis. In fact, it is precisely this substitution of a triangular for an oval handle, which characterizes the crux ansata of India, or at least the figure connected by Indian scholars with the Egyptian symbol of the Key of Life (fig. b, above- on a silver ingot (EDW. THOMAS, in *the Numismatic Chronicle,* vol. iv. (new series), pl. xi.), which reached India by way of Syria and Persia.[63]

The use of the Ancient Egyptian ankh symbol on the feet of Buddha is appropriate in view of the special relationship that has been discovered between Neterian Religion and Buddhism, especially in view of the fact that the ankh symbol is exoterically constructed from a sandal strap, implying the idea of the life giving lotus footed personality.

Above-left- The Ancient Egyptian *Ankh* symbol. Above-right- Ancient Egyptian Sandal symbol

Greeks from the early Christian times said that the Egyptian *Ankh,* ☥ , was "common to the worship of Christ and *Serapis* (Greek-Roman name for Asar). In Roman times, Saint Helena (c. 255-330), the mother of Roman Emperor Constantine-I (Constantine the Great) became a Christian around the time her son became emperor of Rome. Early church historians relate many stories about Helena. One of the stories was that Helena inspired the building of the Church of the Nativity in Bethlehem. Later tradition says that she founded the true cross on which Christ died. This was the *Tau Cross,* **T**, which resembles the Druid crosses. The *Maltese Cross,* ✠, was related to gods and goddesses of Malta before it was adopted by Christianity. One of the most important symbolic references of the Christian cross or "Latin Cross," ♰, is that its vertical axis symbolizes the vertical movement of spiritual discipline (self-effort) which implies true transformation in all areas (mental, spiritual, physical) of life. The vertical movement pierces the horizontal axis of the cross, a symbol of time and space (lateral movement, reincarnation, stagnation, etc.). Other important crosses used by the Christian church were: Early crosses, ♆♱♰; Anchor crosses, ♁♱♱; Monograms of Christ, ☸✤✤; Greek cross, ✛; Celtic cross, ♰; Eastern cross, ☦; Craponee Swastika cross,✚ (similar to the Indian and Persian swastika, 卐).

Originally, the swastika symbol was an ancient sign used to denote the manner in which spiritual energy flows. It is also considered to be a sign of well being and auspiciousness, and can be found in the seals of the Indus Valley Civilization of Pre-Vedic India. It was thus an ancient cosmic or religious symbol used by the Pre-Vedic-Indus, Hindus and Greeks. The Swastika is formed by a cross with the ends of the arms bent at right angles in either a clockwise or a counterclockwise direction, denoting the form of energy being manifested.

Ancient Egyptian *Swastika.*

The picture above is of a fragment from a column 520-500 B.C.E. It was found near the Temple of Aphrodite (Hetheru – Hathor) at Naucratis Egypt. (British Museum) Up to now it has been thought by many researchers that the swastika was not used in Africa. However, this evidence shows its use as well as its compatibility with Kamitan spirituality. (picture by Muata Ashby)

Below-left- Modern rendition of the Tantric Hindu divinity, Ardhanari-Ishvara.

The Hindu divinity, Ardhanari is the image of a half man, half woman personality, standing on the lotus of Creation, with a serpent coming out of the top of the head and an ankh symbol at the genitalia, the loop facing the female side and the cross facing the male side. The Ancient Egyptian divinity, Ra, also has a serpent on his head, symbolizing the climax of the Serpent Power, and an ankh in hand. He is also known to be androgynous, like Ardhanari, as he brought forth the company of gods and goddesses which formed Creation.[64] In the form of Nefertum, Ra emerged from the primeval ocean, sitting on his lotus.

Below-right- the Ancient Egyptian god Ra, the serpent on top of his head and ankh in hand. Far right – Ra in the form of Nefertum

Below – Close-ups

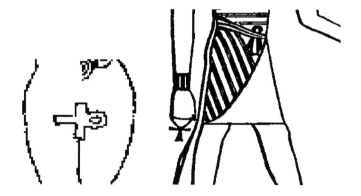

The Divine Wheel

The Dharmacakra (Sanskrit) or Dhammacakka (Pāli), Tibetan *chos.kyi 'khor.lo*, Chinese *fǎlún* 法轮, means "Wheel of Dharma." This symbol represents an auspicious Buddhist icon representing the Buddha's teaching of the path to enlightenment. The term is sometimes also translated as "wheel of doctrine" or "wheel of law." The Dharmacakra symbol makes use of the form of a wheel that has eight or more spokes. One of the oldest Buddhist symbols, it is found in Indian spiritual art from ancient times dating to the reign of the Buddhist king Aśoka. It was used by all Buddhist nations since that time. It is recognized globally as a symbol for Buddhism.

The symbol of the lotus circle was used in Neterianism (Ancient Egyptian Religion). It has 16 petals and symbolizes the path to enlightenment through meditative absorption which is founded upon Maat conscience and righteous action, following the cosmic law. The lotus wheel is at once the multiplicity of the world and the primordial dot that gives rise to all. Sitting

140

on that spot and centering attention on it allows the center of consciousness to emerge.

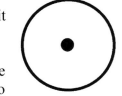

In Neterianism, the symbol of the dot with the outer circle is known as the Sundisk. It is also the symbol of Ra. Like Buddha's halo, Ra makes use of the Sundisk as his halo. The Sundisk symbolizes enlightenment as well as dynamic power. Just as Buddhas enlightenment protects him from the harassment from demons and desires, so too the Ra Akhu or divine spiritual light of the Sundisk protects the enlightened Neterian initiate.

The Pose of Peace
There are other forms of Buddhist and Neterian iconography that are compatible. Below left- Bodhisattva of Western Tibet in Abhaya mudra (upraised right hand in sign of peace) -with exposed right breast. Below right-Ancient Egyptian goddess in the same pose.

The Buddha, Heru and the Ankh, Pyramid and the Lion

The following Stele of Buddha contains some elements that bear strong resemblance to Ancient Egyptian iconography.

Stele of Buddha With two smaller Buddhas and lions

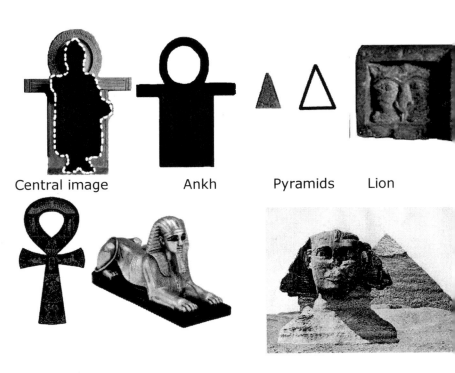

Central image   Ankh   Pyramids   Lion

Egyptian ankh   Sphinx

Great Sphinx and Pyramid

Stele of Heru commonly called Cippi, Reveals power of Heru, standing on two crocodiles (Aspects of himself)

The lions on the bottom corners of the Buddha stele refer to the idea that Buddha belongs to the 'lion clan,' which is known as the Shakyas. This is why he is given the title *"Shakyamuni,"* meaning the silent lion (muni - silent). Heru in Kamit is the "Lord of the two Horizons" or *Heru Akhuti.* He is the beginning, the dawn and the end, the setting sun. That power to achieve mastery of the world and the heavens is contained in the lion power which is Heru himself as the perfected human being who has attained self-mastery in the form of the Great Sphinx under the name: *HerumAkhet.*

The Spiritual Eyes

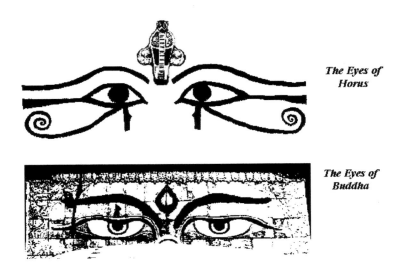

The Eyes of
Horus

The Eyes of
Buddha

Top: The Eyes of Heru (Ancient Egypt), Bottom: The Eyes of Buddha. The right eye symbolizes the sun,☉, and the left eye symbolizes the moon, ☾.

The Spiritual Eyes symbolize the attainment of divine consciousness. The left eye symbolizes inner vision or mental subtlety and enlightenment, the moon, and the right eye symbolizes the power of the spirit, the sun. Both together they represent the attainment of unitary, complete vision and power over the physical and spiritual realms. The symbolism is the same in Ancient Egypt with the eyes of Heru, the eyes of the god Krishna and the god Buddha, and also as shown in this text, the Upanishads state that the eyes of Brahman are also the "Sun and Moon."

The Philosophy of The Witnessing Inner Self in Ancient Egypt and Indian Buddhism

Wakefulness vigilant- *Snehas*

13. He the One Watcher who neither slumbers
   nor sleeps.
                       - Ancient Egyptian Hymns of Amun

Many thousands of years prior to the development of the *Sakshin Buddhi* concept in Vedanta philosophy and the *Mindfulness* concept of Buddhism, the concept of the *witnessing consciousness* was understood in Ancient Egypt. This watcher or witnessing consciousness is related to three other important utterances (33-34), which explain the relationship between the witnessing consciousness of the mind, the perceptions through the senses and the physical world. Here we will focus on understanding the watcher or witnessing consciousness, which is the innermost essence of the human mind.

The Self is the eternal and silent witness to all that goes on in the mind of every human being. It is the mind, composed of memories and desires stored in the subconscious and unconscious, which believes itself to be real and independent. But when you begin to ask "Who is this that I call me?" you begin to discover that you cannot find any "me." Is "me" the person I was at five years of age? At twenty? Or am I the person I see in the mirror today? Am I the person I will be in ten years from now or am I the person I was 500 or 1000 years ago in a different incarnation?[65] Where is "me"? Is "me" the body? Am "I" the legs, or am "I" the heart? Am "I" the brain? People have lost half their brain and continue to live, not in a vegetable state but as human beings, with consciousness. Since body parts can be lost or transplanted, these cannot be "me." What does this all mean?[66]

> *33. He whose name is hidden is Amun, Ra belongeth*
> *to him as His face, and the body is Ptah.*
> *34. Their cities are established on earth forever,*
> *Waset, Anu, Hetkaptah.*
> *-Ancient Egyptian Hymns of Amun*

In Kamitan mysticism, Amun, the Self, is the "hidden" essence of all things. The Sun (Ra) is the radiant and dynamic outward appearance of the hidden made manifest, and also the light of cosmic consciousness, the cosmic mind or that through which consciousness projects. In this aspect, Ptah represents the physical world, the solidification or coagulation of the projection of consciousness (Amun) made manifest. These manifestations are reproduced symbolically on earth in the cities of *KMT* (Egypt) and Waset (Weset) or Newt (Greek - Thebes). Waset was named "Thebes" by the Greeks, who knew it also as *Diospolis* (heavenly city). They also named a sister city in Greece by the same name. Thebes is the city identified in the Old Testament of the Christian Bible as *No* (city), *No-Amon* (city of Amon), *Anu* (city of Ra) and *Hetkaptah* (city of Ptah).

Comparison of Religious Tenets

Basic Religious Tenets of World Religions	Neterianism (African Religion)	Buddhism	Hinduism
1- Ethics and social reform	1-✓	1-✓	1-✓
2-The unity of human kind	2-✓	2-✓	2-✓
3-The equality of the sexes	3-✓	3-✓	3-✓
4-All racial, religious and political prejudices are shunned.	4-✓	4-✓	4-✓
5-Private prayer			
6-Annual fasting periods.	5-✓[67]	5-✓	5-✓
7-Pilgrimage to holy sites.	6-✓	6-✓	6-✓
8-Monetary contributions.	7-×[68]	7-×	7-×[75]
9-Non-violence.	8-✓	8-✓	8-✓
10-World peace through the message of equality and unity.	9-✓	9-✓	9-✓
11-God is unknowable.	10-✓	10-✓	10-✓
12-Immortality is assured	11-×[69]	11-×	11-×[76]
13-Ceremonial leaders are shunned.	12-✓	12-✓	12-✓
14-Spiritual teachings given by revelation through prophets	13-×[70]	13-×	13-×
15-There is a Supreme Being	14-×	14-×	14-×[77]
16-Lesser beings (gods and goddesses)	15-✓	15-✓	15-✓
17-Mysticism	16-✓	16-×[72]	16-✓
18-Yoga philosophy	17-✓	17-✓	17-✓
19-Goddess Spirituality	18-✓	18-✓	18-✓
20- All religions worship the same god	19-✓	19-×[73]	19-✓
	20-✓[71]	20-×[74]	20-×[78]

Epilog: The Counter-Reversion Era, the Passing of Ancient Egyptian Religion into Dormancy, the Creation of Buddhism and the Formation of Western Religion

Henotheism Period

During the sixth century B.C.E. there was a special age in human history, which some authors have termed "Axial age" due to its role in history that may be likened to an axis upon which many events turned. However, that period may be better described as a religious *"Counter-Reversion Era."* The name Counter-Reversion Era was chosen because it describes a time when the religious philosophy of the past [time before that era] was in decline due to the emergence of barbarism and certain religious movements emerged to counter that decline and revert back to the original *perennial philosophy*[79] of religion. During that time, there were several wars of conquest in which several nations in the Middle East developed into conquering forces. Some examples include the Persians and the Assyrians. That period marked a time when the power of Ancient Egypt, which had previously controlled the land areas from present day Sudan to India, at one time in the past, reached its lowest state. Ancient Egypt was under constant siege during that period. However, Egypt did not experience a religious *Counter-Reversion Era*. The Ancient Egyptian religion was a purveyor of the perennial philosophy, the religious tradition of henotheism and panentheism that continued to be practiced openly until the 5th century A.C.E. [1,000 years later] when the Roman Orthodox Christians closed the last Egyptian temples by force.[80] Ancient Egypt had been the beacon of learning and science as well as spiritual wisdom. This is why the ancient pre-Judaic, pre-Christian and pre-Islamic religions had many areas of compatibility with Ancient Egyptian religion and some even included Ancient Egyptian gods and goddesses in their pantheon of divinities. The time prior to the *Counter-Reversion Era* was marked by the practice of henotheism {In philosophy and religion, is a term coined by Max Müller, which means devotion to a single god while accepting the existence of other gods.} and in a more developed format, pantheism {a doctrine identifying the Deity with the universe and its phenomena. Belief in and worship of all gods and goddesses as manifestations of the Supreme Being} and panentheism {the creator is Creation and transcends Creation}.

The Counter-Reversion Era

Part 1:

The *Counter-Reversion Era* covers a period circa the 6th century B.C.E. The philosophies that emerged at that time, such as Pythagoreanism, Buddhism, Jainism, Taoism, and Confucianism had common aspects that hearkened back to and admonished the need to return to a philosophy of mystical spirituality, community service and ethics, such as was taught by the Ancient Egyptians for several thousands of years. Those philosophies, except in Greece, developed in a personalized form, with a personal leader in he form of a realized and or ascended master at its center, as opposed to the priestly format of Ancient Egypt. In other words, the degradation of humanity in the Middle East, due to strife, caused a desire for spirituality that was more personality based instead of mystically based. Ancient Egyptian religion was originally personality based [Ex. God Ra, Osiris or Isis]; however, those personalities did not interfere with the capacity for the practitioners to attain high religious development since the systems introduced by those personalities were based on mystical philosophy with henotheistic components. Therefore, even though the religions that came in during the *Counter-Reversion Era* had specific founding teachers [personalities upon which the religions were based: *Pythagoras, Buddha, Mahavira, Lao-Tzu, Confucius*], whose philosophies pointed to mysticism and the perennial philosophy that has existed before and led people to turn away from violence and towards cooperative peaceful coexistence and a personal quest for enlightenment by discovering the nature of self which transcends the phenomenal and which is essentially a part of the immortal, transcendental Divine, concepts that predated the inception of the new religions and philosophies.

Judaism was practiced in ancient times to the extent that the Torah [the main original Jewish religious texts] is believed by scholars to have been read publicly since the time of Ezra (c. 450 B.C.E. –after the *Counter-Reversion Era*).[81] However, at that time, Judaism did not have the Rabbinical Jewish principles of absolute monotheism as we may understand its practice today which rejects all gods and recognizes only one. At this time Judaism accepted the henotheistic concept which means devotion to a single god while accepting the existence of other gods. However, after the Babylonian conquest of Jerusalem, the Jews (people of Judah, part of the land ruled by the kings Saul, David, Solomon and their descendants)[82] scattered to Egypt and to Babylonia. It seems also contradictory that the Jews who practice the Passover ritual and who commemorate being freed from captivity in Egypt should seek refuge in that same country. Nevertheless, the Egyptian Jews continued to practice the earlier form of Judaism but the Babylonian Jews started to innovate the philosophical tenets of Judaism as a reaction to the debacle caused by the Babylonian destruction of Jerusalem and the Jewish Temple in 586 B.C.E.[83] It is possible that the Babylonian Jews could have come into contact with practitioners of the Zoroastrian tradition at this time. The Babylonian exile period began to set in motion changes in Jewish religion that came to fruition in the next pivotal period of religion in the Middle East that was to have far reaching effects on Christianity and the rest of Western culture in the first and second millenniums A.C.E.

Part 2

Chaos in Ancient Egypt and the Creation of New World Religions including Buddhism

There was an important development in the 6th century B.C.E. that occurred in Egypt at the time when Buddhism emerged. It may be termed "Counter-Reversion Era" since the new religions were trying to counter the chaos caused by barbarian cultures which were disrupting the previous age-old form of spirituality that had persisted previously for thousands of years. Prior to this era Ancient Egypt has been the Holy Land for many peoples; they looked up to Ancient Egypt and a paragon of religious wisdom and spiritual practice. However, that was changing due to the invasions that brought chaos to Egypt and much of the ancient world.

Cambyses II (reigned 529-522 BC), the king of Persia, led an expedition to conquer Egypt, which at the time was the sole independent kingdom in the aftermath the conquests of Asia by his father. Cambyses defeated Psamtik III, king of Egypt, and succeeded in conquering Egypt as far south as Nubia, but he failed in later attacks on the Egyptian oasis of Ammonium (now Siwa) and in campaigns in Ethiopia.

The attacks and conquest of Egypt by the Persians caused an extensive displacements of the Egyptian population. It was at this time that some of the Priests and Priestesses were forced out of the Temples due to fires set by the armies of the Persians. Also, many Egyptians were forcibly taken as slave workers to Persia and other parts of Asia Minor to build monuments and Temples for the Persians in those areas.[84][85] It is during this time that the most powerful and influential philosophies of the ancient world came into being. These included:

- Buddhism   6th century B.C.E.
- Pythagoreanism   6th century B.C.E.
- Taoism   6th century B.C.E.
- Confucianism   6th century B.C.E.
- Zoroastrianism   6th century B.C.E.
- Jainism   6th century B.C.E.

The Ancient Egyptians had been attacked and the country taken over by foreigners twice before. The first time was the Hyksos invasion, which precipitated the "Second Intermediate Period," and the second time was the invasion of the Assyrians which was put down by the Nubians. However, the records indicate[86] that the viciousness of the attack and conquest by the Persians was so severe that it prompted a migration of Ancient Egyptians not only to Asia Minor, but also to India, Europe and other parts of Africa, including Nubia to the south, and West Africa also. Therefore, a causal connection can be drawn between the events in Egypt and the events in other parts of the ancient world. The surviving culture of Egypt was severely weakened after the Persian conquest, so much so that after a brief reestablishment of Egyptian rule by Egyptians, they were conquered again by the Greeks, who themselves had conquered the Persians. This period brought some stability to Egypt as the Greeks allowed the

Ancient Egyptian religion to continue under their auspices, and the connection that had been established between other countries and Egypt through the Egyptians that had migrated out of Egypt 200 years earlier[87] during the invasion of Cambyses and the open relations fostered by the Ptolemaic rulers continued into a new phase. Now Egypt was fully opened to the spiritual seekers of the ancient world, and they flocked to the land of the Pyramids.

In this respect some researchers have noted the similarities between the Ancient Egyptian and Buddhist iconographies and point to these, and the evidences of philosophical correlations and evidences of contact along with the images of Buddha himself, as sufficient proof to show that Buddha was an African-Egyptian priest. Indeed, even when we consider that no images of Buddha were allowed until the 1st century B.C.E. with the advent of Mahayana Buddhism, the images that appear even at that time, and later, up to the present day, bear a resemblance to the Kamitan-Kushitic forms of imagery and human appearance. There is a resemblance especially in the depiction of the hair and certain aspects of the physiognomy, in particular the nose and eye region of the face. It is curly or in locks, a form that was originated in ancient Kamit.

Conclusion

We, along with some Indian researchers, have presented evidences, in addition to evidences of correlation in the iconography and philosophy, which prove that there was a strong connection between Memphite Theology {Memphitism} and the early Buddhism, so I would say that it is reasonable to say that Buddhism and its creators were impelled by Ancient Egyptian religion just as the Confucians, the Pythagoreans, the Taoists and the other religions that emerged around the same time as the Persian invasion. However, it is not the same as saying that the modern practice of Buddhism is the same as what the Ancient Egyptians were doing. Some of the differences are obvious and others not so obvious. In order to discern the more subtle nuances a deeper study of the philosophies is required and that would follow by entering into depth studies in other volumes in this series. In any case, the close correlations and common history shared by Buddhism and Neterianism indicates that they are compatible spiritual traditions.

Summary

Thus, in the view of this researcher the evidences presented in this volume of supportable matching cultural factors and evidence of contact between Ancient Egyptian Neterianism and Indian Buddhism and the nature of those contacts, show substantial borrowings from Ancient Egyptian Neterianism to Indian Buddhism with regard to the factors of cultural expression. These are sufficient to confidently conclude that:

1. Ancient Egyptian civilization was already established, thousands of years before Ancient Indian culture began.
2. Upon examination of the Kamitan Neterian (especially Memphite Theology) Categories of Cultural Expression and the Ancient Indian Buddhist Categories of Cultural Expressions it is clear that the Factors of the categories match closely in the two cultures.
3. So it is possible to say that Indian Buddhism drew from Ancient Egyptian Neterianism in the creation of customs and traditions as well as religion and philosophy over a substantial period of the Indian Buddhist early history.
4. Indian Buddhism is a continuation of Nubian-Kamitan Memphite Neterian (religion) culture albeit transformed through history and influenced by outside cultures in many respects. However, the fundamental categories and principles of Indian Buddhist culture match those of Ancient Egyptian Neterian Religion.

NOTES

[1] Random House Encyclopedia Copyright (C) 1983,1990

[2] *Doshi, Saryu, Editor-Indian Council for Cultural Relations India and Egypt: Influences and Interactions 1993*

[3] *Pottery Headrests from Narsipur Sangam,* F.R. Allchin, *Studies in Indian Prehistory*, D. Sen and A.K. Ghosh, eds., Calcutta, 1966, pp. 58-63

[4] *Chanudaro Excavations, 1935-36* E.J.H. Mackay, American Oriental Society, New Heaven, 19443, pp. 25 and 220, pl. XCII, 38

[5] Nagaraja Rao, op. Cit., p. 144; also Allchin, op. Cit.

[6] Ibid.

[7] From Wikipedia Encyclopedia

[8] From Wikipedia Encyclopedia

[9] From Wikipedia Encyclopedia

[10] From Wikipedia Encyclopedia

[11] From Wikipedia Encyclopedia

[12] (*Daruma Daishi* in Japanese, Da mo in China; Bodhidharma was the third prince of the Chola Dynasty, descended from the North Indian Cholas, which ruled the area of Kanchipuram in the South) From Wikipedia Encyclopedia

[13] From Wikipedia Encyclopedia

[14] From Wikipedia encyclopedia

[15] From Wikipedia encyclopedia

[16] From Wikipedia encyclopedia

[17] **Clement of Alexandria** (Titus Flavius Clemens), was the first member of the Church of Alexandria to be more than a name, and one of its most distinguished teachers. He was born about the middle of the 2nd century, and died between 211 and 216.

[18] Ancient Egyptian priests and priestesses

[19] Source: *Wikipedia, the free encyclopedia © 2001-2006*

[20] ibid

[21] major temple and city in Ancient Egypt.

[22] See previous note.

[23] See previous note.

[24] See the book *Memphite Theology* by Muata Ashby

[25] *In much the same way as the term Heru refers to anyone who has attained "Heruhood" or the term Christ refers to anyone who has attained "Christhood", the term Buddha refers to any one who has attained the state of enlightenment. In this context there have been many male and female Christs and Buddhas throughout history.

[26] See the book *Glorious Light Meditation* and *Anunian Theology* by Muata Ashby

[27] See the book *Resurrecting Osiris* by Muata Ashby

[28] *Memphite Theology: The Hidden Properties of Matter,* Muata Ashby 1997

[29] ibid.

[30] *The People of South Asia* Edited by J. R. Lukacs, ed., Chapter 3, *Biological anthropology of Bronze Age[30] Harappans: new perspectives*, Pratap C. Dutta

[31] *Doshi, Saryu, Editor-Indian Council for Cultural Relations India and Egypt: Influences and Interactions* 1993

[32] *A Concise Encyclopedia of Hinduism,* by Klaus K. Klostermaier

[33] Compton's Interactive Encyclopedia Copyright (c) 1994, 1995

[34] *A Concise Encyclopedia of Hinduism,* by Klaus K. Klostermaier

[35] Tradition founded by Mahavira – 6th century B.C.E.

[36] Worship of Shiva

[37] Worship of Vishnu and his forms.

[38] Related to the goddess, Shakti, it is the worship of the cosmic energy.

[39] Spiritual traditions which uses male and female sexual symbolism and goddess worship as metaphors for non-dual philosophy.

[40] Mystical technologies

[41] Dualistic philosophy used to discover non-dual consciousness and enlightenment.

[42] all of these taken together constitute "Hinduism" – Sanatana Dharma - in the modern interpretation of the word

[43] Excerpted from *Compton's Interactive Encyclopedia.* Copyright (c) 1994, 1995 Compton's NewMedia, Inc. All Rights Reserved

[44] Interviewed followers of the International Society For Krishna Consciousness 2000 A.C.E.

[45] H.G. Rawlinson, *Intercourse Between India and the Western World,* Cambridge, 1916, pp. 93-94

[46] Now at the Petrie Museum in London (UC nos. 8816, 8931, 8788)

[47] Flinders Petrie, *Memphis,* vol. 1, London 1909, pp. 16-17 pl. XXXIX.

[48] J.C. Harke, "The Indian Terracottas from Ancient Memphis: Are they really Indian?, *Dr. Debala Mitra Volume,* Delhi, 1991, pp. 55-61

[49] Charles Elliot, *Hinduism and Buddhism,* vol. III, London, 1954, pp. 93-94

[50] "Asoka," Microsoft (R) Encarta Copyright (c) 1994 Funk & Wagnall's Corporation. "Ashoka," Random House Encyclopedia Copyright (C) 1983,1990 by Random House Inc.

[51] K. G. Krishnan, Uttankita Sanskrit Vidya Arangnya Epigraphs, vol. II, Mysore, 1989, pp 42 ff

[52] H. G. Rawlison, *Intercourse between India and the Western World,* Cambridge, 1916, p. 92.

[53] Krishnan, op. cit., pp. 17-18

[54] Rawlison, op. cit., p. 93

[55] Copyright © 1995 Helicon Publishing Ltd Encyclopedia

[56] *Travelers Guide to Ancient Egypt,* John Anthony West

[57] *In Search of the Cradle of Civilization,* 1995, co-authored by Georg Feuerstein, David Frawley, and Subhash Kak.

[58] *A Concise Encyclopedia of Hinduism,* by Klaus K. Klostermaier

[59] For more details on the philosophy of Maat see the books *The 42 Principles of Maat and the Philosophy of Righteous Action* and *The Egyptian Book of the Dead* by Muata Ashby

[60] *The Power of Myth,* Joseph Campbell

[61] *The Mythic Image,* Joseph Campbell

[62] From more details see the book **Christian Yoga** by Dr. Muata Ashby.

[63] *The Migration of Symbols,* Count Goblet D' Alviella, 1894

[64] From more details see the book ***Egyptian Yoga Vol. 1*** by Dr. Muata Ashby.

[65] Reincarnation has been documented and verified by 20th century parapshychologists and past life regressionists.

[66] For a more detailed study of the Kamitan teachings related to the "Witnessing Self" see the book Egyptian Yoga Vol. 2.

[67] Private prayer is enjoined in African religion but also ritual and mass programs as well. The same is true for Hinduism and Buddhism.

[68] Pilgrimage to Kamit and its holy sites.

[69] God is unknowable to those who remain at the lower levels of human consciousness.

[70] Priests and Priestesses are necessary to lead people. In an attempt to avoid messianic leaders som religions have shunned leadership altogether but this is only an official statement but it is not true in practice as there always needs to be someone to explain the teachings, otherwise how would the faith be transmitted? So in Islam, which also shuns leaders, there are Imams, in Sikhism, which also shuns gurus, there are revered leaders, and so too it is in Bahai. The same is true for Hinduism and Buddhism.

[71] Ancient Egyptian religion contains both orthodox and mystical aspects within the same system of theology, therefore it is personal as well as impersonal and so can accommodate the needs of the masses as well as the needs of the mystics.

[72] Some sects of Buddhism believe in Buddha as a being that manifests in the form of Buddha Consciousness in all things. This is in all respects equal to the Kamitan and Hindu mystic traditions but it is not common to all Buddhist traditions.

[73] Not all Buddhist sects affirm the Goddess as an enlightener. Some Tantric sects do however.

[74] Remember that there are two main sects, not including Tantrism, Lamaism and others. The orthodox meditate on pure consciousness while the lay Buddhists see Buddha as a divinity. However, mystics in Buddhism would agree that they "worship" the same divinity as all other human beings do.

[75] Pilgrimage to Hindu holy sites

[76] God is unknowable to those who remain at the lower levels of human consciousness.

[77] Some orthodox sects of Hinduism believe that their tradition was started by an avatar and that this is a special revelation. However, the Hindu mystics derive insight through teachers and direct insight through spiritual disciplines.

[78] Some sects of Hinduism believe in an exclusive, personal god (ex. Krishna Consciousness movement). They do not believe in god as impersonal consciousness. However, mystics in Hinduism would agree that they "worship" the same divinity as all other human beings do.

79 The Perennial Philosophy (Latin philosophia perennis) is the idea that a universal set of truths common to all people and cultures exists. The term was first used by the German mathematician and philosopher Gottfried Leibniz to designate the common, eternal philosophy that underlies all religious movements, in particular the mystical streams within them. The term was later popularized by Aldous Huxley in his 1945 book The Perennial Philosophy. The term "perennial philosophy" has also been used to translate the concept of the "eternal or perennial truth" in the Sanskrit Sanatana Dharma.

The concept of perennial philosophy is the fundamental tenet of the Traditionalist School, formalized in the writings of 20th century metaphysicians René Guénon and Frithjof Schuon. The Indian scholar and writer Ananda Coomaraswamy, associated with the Traditionalists, also wrote extensively about the perennial philosophy. http://en.wikipedia.org/wiki/Perennial_philosophy

[80] *African Origins of Civilization*, by Muata Ashby, *Mystical Journey From Jesus to Christ*, by Muata Ashby

81 Essential Judiasm: A Complete Guide to Beliefs, Customs and Rituals by George Robinson (Pocket Books, 2000). "Torah, Torah, Torah: The Unfolding of a Tradition." Judaism for Dummies (Hungry Minds, 2001). Tracey R. Rich, "Torah." Judaism 101 (1995-99).

82 While the term Jewish is used largely as a religious or and ethnic designation it is actually a religious designation or name.

83 Jewish Life in Ancient Egypt by Edward Bleiberg for the Brooklyn Museum 2002

[84] Cambyses II (d. 522 BC), son of Cyrus the Great and King of Persia (529-522 BC), his main achievement was the conquest of Egypt. His other campaigns failed and turned him from a benevolent to a harsh ruler. He died in battle in Syria. (Random House Encyclopedia Copyright (C) 1983,1990)

[85] *The African Origins of Civilization*, Cheikh Anta Diop, 1974

[86] *History of Herodotus*, *Reliefs on the palace of Ashurbanipal*

[87] Review section entitled **Paleoanthropology shows a connection between Ancient Egypt, Ancient Persia and Ancient India**

Bibliography

1. A Concise Encyclopedia of Hinduism, by Klaus K. Klostermaier
2. A Concise History of Buddhism by Andrew Skilton
3. A Sanskrit-English Dictionary, Monier Williams, p. 528
4. African Presence in Early Asia edited by Ivan Van Sertima and Runoko Rashidi
5. African Origins of Civilization by Muata Ashby
6. Am I a Hindu?: the Hinduism Primer by Ed. Viswanathan
7. Art - Culture of India and Egypt, the author S. M El Mansouri
8. Bardo Teachings by Lama Lodo
9. Based on the new discoveries at the city of Mehrgarh - Indus Valley
10. Buddha: the Intelligent Heart by Alistair Shearer
11. Buddha: the Intelligent Heart" by Alistair Shearer
12. Charles Elliot, Hinduism and Buddhism, vol. III, London, 1954, pp. 93-94
13. Civilizations of the Indus Valley and Beyond, Sir Mortimer Wheeler.
14. Comparative Mythology, Jaan Puhvel
15. Connection of Egypt with India, F.W.H. Migeod, Man, vol. 24, no. 118, London, 1924, p. 160
16. Dancing Wu Li Masters by Gary Zukov
17. Dangerous Friend: A Teacher-Student Relationship in Vajrayana Buddhism by Rig'dzin Dorje
18. Death, Intermediate State and Rebirth in Tibetan Buddhism by Lati Rinbochay & Jeffrey Hopkins
19. Decline and Fall of Buddhism by Dr. K. Jamanadas

20. Doshi, Saryu, Editor-Indian Council for Cultural Relations India and Egypt: Influences and Interactions 1993
21. Dutta, P. C. 1984. Biological anthropology of Bronze Ace. Harappans: new perspectives. In The People of South Asia.
22. Egypt and India by Muata Ashby
23. Egyptian Yoga Postures of the Gods and Goddesses by Muata Ashby
24. Eliade, Yoga: Immortality and Freedom, Bollingen Series LVI, 2nd edn. (Princeton: Princeton University Press, 1969), PP. 370-372 ("Patanjali and the Texts of Classic Yoga").
25. Encyclopedia of Mysticism and Mystery Religions by John Ferguson
26. Encyclopedic Dictionary of Yoga by Georg Feurstein
27. Encyclopedic Dictionary of Yoga" by Georg Feurstein
28. Ferdmand's Handbook to the World's Religions
29. Feuerstein, Georg, The Shambhala Encyclopedia of Yoga 1997
30. Gods of India, p. 35. Martin
31. H. G. Rawlinson, Intercourse between India and the Western World, Cambridge
32. Hatha-Yoga-Pradipika, The Shambhala Encyclopedia of Yoga by Georg Feuerstein, Ph. D.
33. Hatha Yoga The Hidden Language by Swami Sivananda Radha
34. Hindu Myths by Wendy O'Flaherty
35. Hindu Myths" by Wendy O'Flaherty
36. In Search of the Cradle of Civilization, 1995, co-authored by Georg Feuerstein, David Frawley, and Subhash Kak.
37. Indian Myth and Legend, Donald A. Mckenzie
38. Indian Mythology, Veronica Ions

39. Integral Yoga by Swami Jyotirmayananda
40. International Society for Krishna Consciousness
41. J.C.Harke, "The Indian Terracottas from Ancient Memphis: Are they really Indian?, Dr. Debala Mitra Volume, Delhi, 1991, pp. 55-61
42. Jnana Yoga by Swami Jyotirmayananda
43. Jnana Yoga" by Swami Jyotirmayananda
44. K. G. Krishnan, Uttankita Sanskrit Vidya Arangnya Epigraphs, vol. II, Mysore, 1989, pp 42 ff
45. Kosambi, D. D., Ancient India a History of its Culture and Civilisation, 1965.
46. Kundalini by Gopi Krishna
47. Kundalini" by Gopi Krishna
48. Living Yoga, Georg Feuerstein, Stephan Bodian, with the staff of Yoga Journal
49. Macdonell, A. A., Vedic Mythology, Delhi: Motilal Banarsidass, 1974.
50. Mackenzie, Donald A., Indian Myth and Legend, London 1913
51. Mansouri El S. M., Art - Culture of India and Egypt 1959
52. Monier-Williams, Indian Wisdom, p. 19.
53. Mystical spirituality texts of India.
54. Mysticism of Hindu Gods and Goddesses by Swami Jyotirmayananda
55. Mysticism of the Mahabharata Swami Jyotirmayananda 1993
56. Pottery Headrests from Narsipur Sangam, F.R. Allchin, Studies in Indian Prehistory, D. Sen and A.K. Ghosh, eds., Calcutta, 1966, pp. 58-63
57. Prehistoric India and Ancient Egypt 1956 Ray, Kumar Sudhansu
58. Proof of Vedic Culture's Global Existence by Steven Knapp
59. Raja Yoga Sutras, Swami Jyotirmayananda

60. Rashidi, Runoko and Van Sertima, Ivan, Editors African Presence in Early Asia 1985-1995
61. Ray, Kumar Sudhansu, Prehistoric India and Ancient Egypt 1956
62. Reading Buddhist Art by Meher McArthur
63. Rig Veda by Aryan and Indian Sages
64. SADHANA by Swami Sivananda
65. SADHANA" by Swami Sivananda
66. Sanskrit Keys to the Wisdom Religion, by Judith Tyberg
67. Search for the Buddha by Charles Allen
68. The Bhagavad Gita" translated by Antonio DE Nicola
69. The Bhagavad Gita" translated by Swami Jyotirmayananda
70. The Great Book of Tantra" by Indra Sinha
71. The Living Gita by Swami Satchidananda 3rd ed. 1997
72. The RIG VEDA Ralph T.H. Griffith, translator 1889
73. The Sivananda Companion to Yoga, Lucy Lidell, Narayani, Giris Rabinovitch)
74. The Story of Buddhism by Donald S. Lopez Jr.
75. The Story of Islam
76. The Tantric Way by Ajit Mookerjee and Madhu Khanna
77. The Tantric Way" by Ajit Mookerjee and Madhu Khanna
78. The Tao of Physics, Fritjof Capra
79. The Tibetan Book of the Dead by Francesca Fremantle & Chogyam Trungpa
80. The Upanishads, Max Muller, translator
81. The Upanishads: Breath of the Eternal, Swami Prabhavananda and Frederick Manchester
82. The Upanishads" by Swami Prabhavananda
83. The Yoga of Wisdom, Swami Jyotirmayananda

84. Vedic Aryans and the Origins of Civilization by David Frawley
85. Vivekacudamani" by Shankaracarya
86. Way of Tibetan Buddhism by Lama Jampa Thaye
87. Yoga Vasistha Ramayana translated by Swami Jyotirmayananda
88. Yoga Vasistha Vol. I by Sage Valmiki -Translation by Swami Jyotirmayananda
89. Yoga Vasistha, Nirvana Prakarana Swami Jyotirmayananda, 1998

Index

Other Books From C M Books

P.O.Box 570459
Miami, Florida, 33257
(305) 378-6253 Fax: (305) 378-6253

This book is part of a series on the study and practice of Ancient Egyptian Yoga and Mystical Spirituality based on the writings of Dr. Muata Abhaya Ashby. They are also part of the Egyptian Yoga Course provided by the Sema Institute of Yoga. Below you will find a listing of the other books in this series. For more information send for the Egyptian Yoga Book-Audio-Video Catalog or the Egyptian Yoga Course Catalog.

Now you can study the teachings of Egyptian and Indian Yoga wisdom and Spirituality with the Egyptian Yoga Mystical Spirituality Series. The Egyptian Yoga Series takes you through the Initiation process and lead you to understand the mysteries of the soul and the Divine and to attain the highest goal of life: ENLIGHTENMENT. The *Egyptian Yoga Series*, takes you on an in depth study of Ancient Egyptian mythology and their inner mystical meaning. Each Book is prepared for the serious student of the mystical sciences and provides a study of the teachings along with exercises, assignments and projects to make the teachings understood and effective in real life. The Series is part of the Egyptian Yoga course but may be purchased even if you are not taking the course. The series is ideal for study groups.

Prices subject to change.

1.   EGYPTIAN YOGA: THE PHILOSOPHY OF ENLIGHTENMENT An original, fully illustrated work, including hieroglyphs, detailing the meaning of the Egyptian mysteries, tantric yoga, psycho-spiritual and physical exercises. Egyptian Yoga is a guide to the practice of the highest spiritual philosophy which leads to absolute freedom

from human misery and to immortality. It is well known by scholars that Egyptian philosophy is the basis of Western and Middle Eastern religious philosophies such as *Christianity, Islam, Judaism,* the *Kabala,* and Greek philosophy, but what about Indian philosophy, Yoga and Taoism? What were the original teachings? How can they be practiced today? What is the source of pain and suffering in the world and what is the solution? Discover the deepest mysteries of the mind and universe within and outside of your self. 8.5" X 11" ISBN: 1-884564-01-1 Soft $19.95

2.   EGYPTIAN YOGA: African Religion Volume 2-Theban Theology U.S. In this long awaited sequel to *Egyptian Yoga: The Philosophy of Enlightenment* you will take a fascinating and enlightening journey back in time and discover the teachings which constituted the epitome of Ancient Egyptian spiritual wisdom. What are the disciplines which lead to the fulfillment of all desires? Delve into the three states of consciousness (waking, dream and deep sleep) and the fourth state which transcends them all, Neberdjer, "The Absolute." These teachings of the city of Waset (Thebes) were the crowning achievement of the Sages of Ancient Egypt. They establish the standard mystical keys for understanding the profound mystical symbolism of the Triad of human consciousness. ISBN 1-884564-39-9 $23.95

3.   THE KEMETIC DIET: GUIDE TO HEALTH, DIET AND FASTING Health issues have always been important to human beings since the beginning of time. The earliest records of history show that the art of healing was held in high esteem since the time of Ancient Egypt. In the early 20th century, medical doctors had almost attained the status of sainthood by the promotion of the idea that they alone were "scientists" while other healing modalities and traditional healers who did not follow the "scientific method' were nothing but superstitious, ignorant charlatans who at best would take the money of their clients and at worst kill them with the

unscientific "snake oils" and "irrational theories". In the late 20th century, the failure of the modern medical establishment's ability to lead the general public to good health, promoted the move by many in society towards "alternative medicine". Alternative medicine disciplines are those healing modalities which do not adhere to the philosophy of allopathic medicine. Allopathic medicine is what medical doctors practice by an large. It is the theory that disease is caused by agencies outside the body such as bacteria, viruses or physical means which affect the body. These can therefore be treated by medicines and therapies The natural healing method began in the absence of extensive technologies with the idea that all the answers for health may be found in nature or rather, the deviation from nature. Therefore, the health of the body can be restored by correcting the aberration and thereby restoring balance. This is the area that will be covered in this volume. Allopathic techniques have their place in the art of healing. However, we should not forget that the body is a grand achievement of the spirit and built into it is the capacity to maintain itself and heal itself. Ashby, Muata ISBN: 1-884564-49-6 $28.95

4.   INITIATION INTO EGYPTIAN YOGA Shedy: Spiritual discipline or program, to go deeply into the mysteries, to study the mystery teachings and literature profoundly, to penetrate the mysteries. You will learn about the mysteries of initiation into the teachings and practice of Yoga and how to become an Initiate of the mystical sciences. This insightful manual is the first in a series which introduces you to the goals of daily spiritual and yoga practices: Meditation, Diet, Words of Power and the ancient wisdom teachings.   8.5" X 11" ISBN 1-884564-02-X   Soft Cover $24.95 U.S.

5.   *THE AFRICAN ORIGINS OF CIVILIZATION, RELIGION AND YOGA SPIRITUALITY AND ETHICS PHILOSOPHY* HARD COVER EDITION Part 1, Part 2, Part 3 in one volume 683 Pages Hard Cover First Edition Three volumes in one. Over the past several years I have been asked to put together in one volume the most important evidences showing the correlations and common teachings between Kamitan (Ancient Egyptian) culture and religion and that of India. The questions of the history of Ancient Egypt, and the latest archeological evidences showing civilization and culture in

Ancient Egypt and its spread to other countries, has intrigued many scholars as well as mystics over the years. Also, the possibility that Ancient Egyptian Priests and Priestesses migrated to Greece, India and other countries to carry on the traditions of the Ancient Egyptian Mysteries, has been speculated over the years as well. In chapter 1 of the book *Egyptian Yoga The Philosophy of Enlightenment,* 1995, I first introduced the deepest comparison between Ancient Egypt and India that had been brought forth up to that time. Now, in the year 2001 this new book, *THE AFRICAN ORIGINS OF CIVILIZATION, MYSTICAL RELIGION AND YOGA PHILOSOPHY,* more fully explores the motifs, symbols and philosophical correlations between Ancient Egyptian and Indian mysticism and clearly shows not only that Ancient Egypt and India were connected culturally but also spiritually. How does this knowledge help the spiritual aspirant? This discovery has great importance for the Yogis and mystics who follow the philosophy of Ancient Egypt and the mysticism of India. It means that India has a longer history and heritage than was previously understood. It shows that the mysteries of Ancient Egypt were essentially a yoga tradition which did not die but rather developed into the modern day systems of Yoga technology of India. It further shows that African culture developed Yoga Mysticism earlier than any other civilization in history. All of this expands our understanding of the unity of culture and the deep legacy of Yoga, which stretches into the distant past, beyond the Indus Valley civilization, the earliest known high culture in India as well as the Vedic tradition of Aryan culture. Therefore, Yoga culture and mysticism is the oldest known tradition of spiritual development and Indian mysticism is an extension of the Ancient Egyptian mysticism. By understanding the legacy which Ancient Egypt gave to India the mysticism of India is better understood and by comprehending the heritage of Indian Yoga, which is rooted in Ancient Egypt the Mysticism of Ancient Egypt is also better understood. This expanded understanding allows us to prove the underlying kinship of humanity, through the common symbols, motifs and philosophies which are not disparate and confusing teachings but in reality expressions of the same study of truth through metaphysics and mystical realization of Self. (HARD COVER) ISBN: 1-884564-50-X $45.00 U.S.   8 1/2" X 11"

6.   AFRICAN ORIGINS BOOK 1 PART 1 African Origins of African Civilization, Religion, Yoga Mysticism and Ethics Philosophy-Soft Cover $24.95 ISBN: 1-884564-55-0

7.   AFRICAN ORIGINS BOOK 2 PART 2 African Origins of Western Civilization, Religion and Philosophy (Soft) -Soft Cover $24.95 ISBN: 1-884564-56-9

8.   EGYPT AND INDIA AFRICAN ORIGINS OF Eastern Civilization, Religion, Yoga Mysticism and Philosophy-Soft Cover $29.95 (Soft) ISBN: 1-884564-57-7

9.   THE MYSTERIES OF ISIS: **The Ancient Egyptian Philosophy of Self-Realization** - There are several paths to discover the Divine and the mysteries of the higher Self. This volume details the mystery teachings of the goddess Aset (Isis) from Ancient Egypt- the path of wisdom. It includes the teachings of her temple and the disciplines that are enjoined for the initiates of the temple of Aset as they were given in ancient times. Also, this book includes the teachings of the main myths of Aset that lead a human being to spiritual enlightenment and immortality. Through the study of ancient myth and the illumination of initiatic understanding the idea of God is expanded from the mythological comprehension to the metaphysical. Then this metaphysical understanding is related to you, the student, so as to begin understanding your true divine nature. ISBN 1-884564-24-0 $22.99

10.   EGYPTIAN PROVERBS: collection of —Ancient Egyptian Proverbs and Wisdom Teachings -How to live according to MAAT Philosophy. Beginning Meditation. All proverbs are indexed for easy searches. For the first time in one volume, — —Ancient Egyptian Proverbs, wisdom teachings and meditations, fully illustrated with hieroglyphic text and symbols. EGYPTIAN PROVERBS is a unique collection of knowledge and wisdom which you can put into practice today and transform your life. $14.95 U.S   ISBN: 1-884564-00-3

11.   GOD OF LOVE: THE PATH OF DIVINE LOVE The Process of Mystical Transformation and The Path of Divine Love This Volume focuses on the ancient wisdom teachings of "Neter Merri" –the Ancient Egyptian philosophy of Divine Love and how to use them in a scientific process for self-transformation. Love is one of the most powerful human emotions. It is also the source of Divine feeling that unifies God and the individual human being. When love is fragmented and diminished by egoism the Divine connection is lost. The Ancient tradition of Neter Merri leads human beings back to their Divine connection, allowing them to discover their innate glorious self that is actually Divine and immortal. This volume will detail the process of transformation from ordinary consciousness to cosmic consciousness through the integrated practice of the teachings and the path of Devotional Love toward the Divine. 5.5"x 8.5" ISBN 1-884564-11-9 $22.95

12.   INTRODUCTION TO MAAT PHILOSOPHY: Spiritual Enlightenment Through the Path of Virtue   Known as Karma Yoga in India, the teachings of MAAT for living virtuously and with orderly wisdom are explained and the student is to begin practicing the precepts of Maat in daily life so as to promote the process of purification of the heart in preparation for the judgment of the soul. This judgment will be understood not as an event that will occur at the time of death but as an event that occurs continuously, at every moment in the life of the individual. The student will learn how to become allied with the forces of the Higher Self and to thereby begin cleansing the mind (heart) of impurities so as to attain a higher vision of reality. ISBN 1-884564-20-8 $22.99

13.   MEDITATION The Ancient Egyptian Path to Enlightenment Many people do not know about the rich history of meditation practice in Ancient Egypt. This volume outlines the theory of meditation and presents the Ancient Egyptian Hieroglyphic text which give instruction as to the nature of the mind and its three modes of expression. It also presents the texts which give instruction on the practice of meditation for spiritual Enlightenment and unity with the Divine. This volume allows the reader to begin practicing meditation by explaining, in easy to understand terms, the simplest form of meditation and

working up to the most advanced form which was practiced in ancient times and which is still practiced by yogis around the world in modern times. ISBN 1-884564-27-7 $22.99

14. THE GLORIOUS LIGHT MEDITATION TECHNIQUE OF ANCIENT EGYPT New for the year 2000. This volume is based on the earliest known instruction in history given for the practice of formal meditation. Discovered by Dr. Muata Ashby, it is inscribed on the walls of the Tomb of Seti I in Thebes Egypt. This volume details the philosophy and practice of this unique system of meditation originated in Ancient Egypt and the earliest practice of meditation known in the world which occurred in the most advanced African Culture. ISBN: 1-884564-15-1 $16.95 (PB)

15. THE SERPENT POWER: The Ancient Egyptian Mystical Wisdom of the Inner Life Force.   This Volume specifically deals with the latent life Force energy of the universe and in the human body, its control and sublimation. How to develop the Life Force energy of the subtle body. This Volume will introduce the esoteric wisdom of the science of how virtuous living acts in a subtle and mysterious way to cleanse the latent psychic energy conduits and vortices of the spiritual body. ISBN 1-884564-19-4 $22.95

16. EGYPTIAN YOGA *The Postures of The Gods and Goddesses* Discover the physical postures and exercises practiced thousands of years ago in Ancient Egypt which are today known as Yoga exercises. Discover the history of the postures and how they were transferred from Ancient Egypt in Africa to India through Buddhist Tantrism. Then practice the postures as you discover the mythic teaching that originally gave birth to the postures and was practiced by the Ancient Egyptian priests and priestesses. This work is based on the pictures and teachings from the Creation story of Ra, The Asarian Resurrection Myth and the carvings and reliefs from various Temples in Ancient Egypt 8.5" X 11" ISBN 1-884564-10-0 Soft Cover $21.95   Exercise video $20

17. SACRED SEXUALITY: EGYPTIAN TANTRA YOGA: The Art of Sex Sublimation and Universal Consciousness This Volume will expand on the male and female principles within the human body and in the universe and further detail the

sublimation of sexual energy into spiritual energy. The student will study the deities Min and Hathor, Asar and Aset, Geb and Nut and discover the mystical implications for a practical spiritual discipline. This Volume will also focus on the Tantric aspects of Ancient Egyptian and Indian mysticism, the purpose of sex and the mystical teachings of sexual sublimation which lead to self-knowledge and Enlightenment. 5.5"x 8.5" ISBN 1-884564-03-8 $24.95

18.   AFRICAN RELIGION Volume 4: ASARIAN THEOLOGY: RESURRECTING OSIRIS The path of Mystical Awakening and the Keys to Immortality NEW REVISED AND EXPANDED EDITION! The Ancient Sages created stories based on human and superhuman beings whose struggles, aspirations, needs and desires ultimately lead them to discover their true Self. The myth of Aset, Asar and Heru is no exception in this area. While there is no one source where the entire story may be found, pieces of it are inscribed in various ancient Temples walls, tombs, steles and papyri. For the first time available, the complete myth of Asar, Aset and Heru has been compiled from original Ancient Egyptian, Greek and Coptic Texts. This epic myth has been richly illustrated with reliefs from the Temple of Heru at Edfu, the Temple of Aset at Philae, the Temple of Asar at Abydos, the Temple of Hathor at Denderah and various papyri, inscriptions and reliefs. Discover the myth which inspired the teachings of the *Shetaut Neter* (Egyptian Mystery System - Egyptian Yoga) and the Egyptian Book of Coming Forth By Day. Also, discover the three levels of Ancient Egyptian Religion, how to understand the mysteries of the Duat or Astral World and how to discover the abode of the Supreme in the Amenta, *The Other World* The ancient religion of Asar, Aset and Heru, if properly understood, contains all of the elements necessary to lead the sincere aspirant to attain immortality through inner self-discovery. This volume presents the entire myth and explores the main mystical themes and rituals associated with the myth for understating human existence, creation and the way to achieve spiritual emancipation - *Resurrection.* The Asarian myth is so powerful that it influenced and is still having an effect on the major world religions. Discover the origins and mystical meaning of the Christian Trinity, the Eucharist ritual and the ancient origin of the birthday of Jesus Christ. Soft Cover ISBN: 1-884564-27-5 $24.95

19.   THE EGYPTIAN BOOK OF THE DEAD MYSTICISM OF
THE PERT EM HERU " I Know myself, I know myself, I am
One With God!–From the Pert Em Heru "The Ru Pert em
Heru" or "Ancient Egyptian Book of The Dead," or "Book of
Coming Forth By Day" as it is more popularly known, has
fascinated the world since the successful translation of
Ancient Egyptian hieroglyphic scripture over 150 years ago.
The astonishing writings in it reveal that the Ancient
Egyptians believed in life after death and in an ultimate
destiny to discover the Divine. The elegance and aesthetic
beauty of the hieroglyphic text itself has inspired many see it
as an art form in and of itself. But is there more to it than
that? Did the Ancient Egyptian wisdom contain more than just
aphorisms and hopes of eternal life beyond death? In this
volume Dr. Muata Ashby, the author of over 25 books on
Ancient Egyptian Yoga Philosophy has produced a new
translation of the original texts which uncovers a mystical
teaching underlying the sayings and rituals instituted by the
Ancient Egyptian Sages and Saints. "Once the philosophy of
Ancient Egypt is understood as a mystical tradition instead of
as a religion or primitive mythology, it reveals its secrets
which if practiced today will lead anyone to discover the glory
of spiritual self-discovery. The Pert em Heru is in every way
comparable to the Indian Upanishads or the Tibetan Book of
the Dead $28.95."   ISBN# 1-884564-28-3 Size: 8½" X 11

20.   African Religion VOL. 1- ANUNIAN THEOLOGY THE
MYSTERIES OF RA The Philosophy of Anu and The
Mystical Teachings of The Ancient Egyptian Creation Myth
Discover the mystical teachings contained in the Creation
Myth and the gods and goddesses who brought creation and
human beings into existence. The Creation myth of Anu is the
source of Anunian Theology but also of the other main
theological systems of Ancient Egypt that also influenced
other world religions including Christianity, Hinduism and
Buddhism. The Creation Myth holds the key to understanding
the universe and for attaining spiritual Enlightenment. ISBN:
1-884564-38-0 $19.95

21.   African Religion VOL   3: Memphite Theology:
MYSTERIES OF MIND Mystical Psychology &
Mental Health for Enlightenment and Immortality

based on the Ancient Egyptian Philosophy of Menefer -Mysticism of Ptah, Egyptian Physics and Yoga Metaphysics and the Hidden properties of Matter. This volume uncovers the mystical psychology of the Ancient Egyptian wisdom teachings centering on the philosophy of the Ancient Egyptian city of Menefer (Memphite Theology). How to understand the mind and how to control the senses and lead the mind to health, clarity and mystical self-discovery. This Volume will also go deeper into the philosophy of God as creation and will explore the concepts of modern science and how they correlate with ancient teachings. This Volume will lay the ground work for the understanding of the philosophy of universal consciousness and the initiatic/yogic insight into who or what is God? ISBN 1-884564-07-0 $22.95

22.   AFRICAN RELIGION VOLUME 5: THE GODDESS AND THE EGYPTIAN MYSTERIESTHE PATH OF THE GODDESS THE GODDESS PATH The Secret Forms of the Goddess and the Rituals of Resurrection The Supreme Being may be worshipped as father or as mother. *Ushet Rekhat* or *Mother Worship*, is the spiritual process of worshipping the Divine in the form of the Divine Goddess. It celebrates the most important forms of the Goddess including *Nathor, Maat, Aset, Arat, Amentet and Hathor* and explores their mystical meaning as well as the rising of *Sirius,* the star of Aset (Aset) and the new birth of Hor (Heru). The end of the year is a time of reckoning, reflection and engendering a new or renewed positive movement toward attaining spiritual Enlightenment. The Mother Worship devotional meditation ritual, performed on five days during the month of December and on New Year's Eve, is based on the Ushet Rekhit. During the ceremony, the cosmic forces, symbolized by Sirius - and the constellation of Orion ---, are harnessed through the understanding and devotional attitude of the participant. This propitiation draws the light of wisdom and health to all those who share in the ritual, leading to prosperity and wisdom. $14.95 ISBN 1-884564-18-6

23.   *THE MYSTICAL JOURNEY FROM JESUS TO CHRIST* Discover the ancient Egyptian origins of Christianity before the Catholic Church and learn the mystical teachings given by Jesus to assist all humanity in becoming Christlike. Discover the secret meaning of the Gospels that were discovered in

Egypt. Also discover how and why so many Christian churches came into being. Discover that the Bible still holds the keys to mystical realization even though its original writings were changed by the church. Discover how to practice the original teachings of Christianity which leads to the Kingdom of Heaven. $24.95   ISBN# 1-884564-05-4 size: 8½" X 11"

24.   THE STORY OF ASAR, ASET AND HERU: An Ancient Egyptian Legend (For Children)   Now for the first time, the most ancient myth of Ancient Egypt comes alive for children. Inspired by the books *The Asarian Resurrection: The Ancient Egyptian Bible* and *The Mystical Teachings of The Asarian Resurrection, The Story of Asar, Aset and Heru* is an easy to understand and thrilling tale which inspired the children of Ancient Egypt to aspire to greatness and righteousness.   If you and your child have enjoyed stories like *The Lion King* and *Star Wars you will love The Story of Asar, Aset and Heru.* Also, if you know the story of Jesus and Krishna you will discover than Ancient Egypt had a similar myth and that this myth carries important spiritual teachings for living a fruitful and fulfilling life.   This book may be used along with *The Parents Guide To The Asarian Resurrection Myth: How to Teach Yourself and Your Child the Principles of Universal Mystical Religion.* The guide provides some background to the Asarian Resurrection myth and it also gives insight into the mystical teachings contained in it which you may introduce to your child. It is designed for parents who wish to grow spiritually with their children and it serves as an introduction for those who would like to study the Asarian Resurrection Myth in depth and to practice its teachings. 8.5" X 11" ISBN: 1-884564-31-3 $12.95

25.   THE PARENTS GUIDE TO THE AUSARIAN RESURRECTION MYTH: How to Teach Yourself and Your Child the Principles of Universal Mystical Religion.   This insightful manual brings for the timeless wisdom of the ancient through the Ancient Egyptian myth of Asar, Aset and Heru and the mystical teachings contained in it for parents who want to guide their children to understand and practice the teachings of mystical spirituality. This manual may be used with the children's storybook *The Story of Asar, Aset and*

Heru by Dr. Muata Abhaya Ashby.   ISBN: 1-884564-30-5 $16.95

26.   HEALING THE CRIMINAL HEART. Introduction to Maat Philosophy, Yoga and Spiritual Redemption Through the Path of Virtue   Who is a criminal? Is there such a thing as a criminal heart? What is the source of evil and sinfulness and is there any way to rise above it? Is there redemption for those who have committed sins, even the worst crimes?   Ancient Egyptian mystical psychology holds important answers to these questions. Over ten thousand years ago mystical psychologists, the Sages of Ancient Egypt, studied and charted the human mind and spirit and laid out a path which will lead to spiritual redemption, prosperity and Enlightenment.   This introductory volume brings forth the teachings of the Asarian Resurrection, the most important myth of Ancient Egypt, with relation to the faults of human existence: anger, hatred, greed, lust, animosity, discontent, ignorance, egoism jealousy, bitterness, and a myriad of psycho-spiritual ailments which keep a human being in a state of negativity and adversity ISBN: 1-884564-17-8 $15.95

27.   TEMPLE RITUAL OF THE ANCIENT EGYPTIAN MYSTERIES--THEATER & DRAMA OF THE ANCIENT EGYPTIAN MYSTERIES: Details the practice of the mysteries and ritual program of the temple and the philosophy an practice of the ritual of the mysteries, its purpose and execution. Featuring the Ancient Egyptian stage play-"The Enlightenment of Hathor' Based on an Ancient Egyptian Drama, The original Theater -Mysticism of the Temple of Hetheru 1-884564-14-3 $19.95   By Dr. Muata Ashby

28.   GUIDE TO PRINT ON DEMAND: SELF-PUBLISH FOR PROFIT, SPIRITUAL FULFILLMENT AND SERVICE TO HUMANITY Everyone asks us how we produced so many books in such a short time. Here are the secrets to writing and producing books that uplift humanity and how to get them printed for a fraction of the regular cost. Anyone can become an author even if they have limited funds. All that is necessary is the willingness to learn how the printing and book business work and the desire to follow the special instructions given here for preparing your manuscript format. Then you take your work directly to the non-traditional companies who can produce your books for

less than the traditional book printer can. ISBN: 1-884564-40-2 $16.95 U. S.

29.   Egyptian Mysteries: Vol. 1, Shetaut Neter What are the Mysteries? For thousands of years the spiritual tradition of Ancient Egypt, S*hetaut Neter,* "The Egyptian Mysteries," "The Secret Teachings," have fascinated, tantalized and amazed the world. At one time exalted and recognized as the highest culture of the world, by Africans, Europeans, Asiatics, Hindus, Buddhists and other cultures of the ancient world, in time it was shunned by the emerging orthodox world religions. Its temples desecrated, its philosophy maligned, its tradition spurned, its philosophy dormant in the mystical *Medu Neter,* the mysterious hieroglyphic texts which hold the secret symbolic meaning that has scarcely been discerned up to now. What are the secrets of *Nehast* {spiritual awakening and emancipation, resurrection}. More than just a literal translation, this volume is for awakening to the secret code *Shetitu* of the teaching which was not deciphered by Egyptologists, nor could be understood by ordinary spiritualists. This book is a reinstatement of the original science made available for our times, to the reincarnated followers of Ancient Egyptian culture and the prospect of spiritual freedom to break the bonds of *Khemn,* "ignorance," and slavery to evil forces: *Såaa* . ISBN: 1-884564-41-0 $19.99

30.   EGYPTIAN MYSTERIES VOL 2: Dictionary of Gods and Goddesses This book is about the mystery of neteru, the gods and goddesses of Ancient Egypt (Kamit, Kemet). Neteru means "Gods and Goddesses." But the Neterian teaching of Neteru represents more than the usual limited modern day concept of "divinities" or "spirits." The Neteru of Kamit are also metaphors, cosmic principles and vehicles for the enlightening teachings of Shetaut Neter (Ancient Egyptian-African Religion). Actually they are the elements for one of the most advanced systems of spirituality ever conceived in human history. Understanding the concept of neteru provides a firm basis for spiritual evolution and the pathway for viable culture, peace on earth and a healthy human society.   Why is it important to have gods and goddesses in our lives? In order for spiritual evolution to be possible, once a human being has accepted that there is existence after death and there is a

transcendental being who exists beyond time and space knowledge, human beings need a connection to that which transcends the ordinary experience of human life in time and space and a means to understand the transcendental reality beyond the mundane reality. ISBN: 1-884564-23-2 $21.95

31.   EGYPTIAN MYSTERIES VOL. 3 The Priests and Priestesses of Ancient Egypt This volume details the path of Neterian priesthood, the joys, challenges and rewards of advanced Neterian life, the teachings that allowed the priests and priestesses to manage the most long lived civilization in human history and how that path can be adopted today; for those who want to tread the path of the Clergy of Shetaut Neter. ISBN: 1-884564-53-4 $24.95

32.   The War of Heru and Set: The Struggle of Good and Evil for Control of the World and The Human Soul This volume contains a novelized version of the Asarian Resurrection myth that is based on the actual scriptures presented in the Book Asarian Religion (old name –Resurrecting Osiris). This volume is prepared in the form of a screenplay and can be easily adapted to be used as a stage play. Spiritual seeking is a mythic journey that has many emotional   highs   and   lows,   ecstasies   and depressions, victories and frustrations. This is the War of Life that is played out in the myth as the struggle of Heru and Set and those are mythic characters that represent the human Higher and Lower self. How to understand the war and emerge victorious in the journey o life? The ultimate victory and fulfillment can be experienced, which is not changeable or lost in time. The purpose of myth is to convey the wisdom of life through the story of divinities who show the way to overcome the challenges and foibles of life. In this volume the

feelings and emotions of the characters of the myth have been highlighted to show the deeply rich texture of the Ancient Egyptian myth. This myth contains deep spiritual teachings and insights into the nature of self, of God and the mysteries of life and the means to discover the true meaning of life and thereby achieve the true purpose of life. To become victorious in the battle of life means to become the King (or Queen) of Egypt.Have you seen movies like The Lion King, Hamlet, The Odyssey, or The Little Buddha? These have been some of the most popular movies in modern times. The Sema Institute of Yoga is dedicated to researching and presenting the wisdom and culture of ancient Africa. The Script is designed to be produced as a motion picture but may be addapted for the theater as well. $21.95   copyright 1998 By Dr. Muata Ashby ISBN 1-8840564-44-5

33.   AFRICAN DIONYSUS: FROM EGYPT TO GREECE: The Kamitan Origins of Greek Culture and Religion ISBN: 1-884564-47-X   FROM EGYPT TO GREECE   This insightful manual is a reference to Ancient Egyptian mythology and philosophy and its correlation to what later became known as Greek and Rome mythology and philosophy. It outlines the basic tenets of the mythologies and shoes the ancient origins of Greek culture in Ancient Egypt. This volume also documents the origins of the Greek alphabet in Egypt as well as Greek religion, myth and philosophy of the gods and goddesses from Egypt from the myth of Atlantis and archaic period with the Minoans to the Classical period. This volume also acts as a resource for Colleges students who would like to set up fraternities and sororities based on the original Ancient Egyptian

principles of Sheti and Maat philosophy. ISBN: 1-884564-47-X $22.95 U.S.

34. THE FORTY TWO PRECEPTS OF MAAT, THE PHILOSOPHY OF RIGHTEOUS ACTION AND THE ANCIENT EGYPTIAN WISDOM TEXTS <u>ADVANCED STUDIES</u> This manual is designed for use with the 1998 Maat Philosophy Class conducted by Dr. Muata Ashby. This is a detailed study of Maat Philosophy. It contains a compilation of the 42 laws or precepts of Maat and the corresponding principles which they represent along with the teachings of the ancient Egyptian Sages relating to each. Maat philosophy was the basis of Ancient Egyptian society and government as well as the heart of Ancient Egyptian myth and spirituality. Maat is at once a goddess, a cosmic force and a living social doctrine, which promotes social harmony and thereby paves the way for spiritual evolution in all levels of society. ISBN: 1-884564-48-8 $16.95 U.S.

35. THE SECRET LOTUS: *Poetry of Enlightenment*
Discover the mystical sentiment of the Kemetic teaching as expressed through the poetry of Sebai Muata Ashby. The teaching of spiritual awakening is uniquely experienced when the poetic sensibility is present. This first volume contains the poems written between 1996 and 2003. **1-884564--16 -X $16.99**

Order Form

Telephone orders: Call Toll Free: 1(305) 378-6253. Have your AMEX, Optima, Visa or MasterCard ready.

Fax orders: 1-(305) 378-6253   E-MAIL ADDRESS: Semayoga@aol.com

Postal Orders: Sema Institute of Yoga, P.O. Box 570459, Miami, Fl. 33257. USA.

Please send the following books and / or tapes.

ITEM

_____Cost $_____

_____Cost $_____

_____Cost $_____

_____Cost $_____

_____Cost $_____

                                   Total $_____

Name:_____

Physical Address:_____

City:_____ State:_____ Zip:_____

Sales tax: Please add 6.5% for books shipped to Florida addresses

_____Shipping: $6.50 for first book and .50¢ for each additional

_____Shipping: Outside US $5.00 for first book and $3.00 for each additional

_____Payment:_____

_____Check -Include Driver License #:

        _____

_____Credit card: _____ Visa, _____ MasterCard, _____ Optima,
_____ AMEX.

Card number:_____

Name on card:_____ Exp.

date:_____/_____

Copyright 1995-2005 Dr. R. Muata Abhaya Ashby
Sema Institute of Yoga
P.O.Box 570459, Miami, Florida, 33257
(305) 378-6253 Fax: (305) 378-6253